Victorian
Tasty Dishes

1897

ISBN 978-1-84986-001-7

First published 1897

This digitally printed version 2010 published by

OTCEditions

An imprint of

Orion Trading Company UK Ltd

Registered under the Companies House Act

Number 4968193

© This compilation OTCEditions 2010

Email: Info@otceditions.co.uk

Website: - otceditions.co.uk

This book is in copyright. Sold subject to the conditions that shall not, by way of trade or otherwise, be lent, hired out or resold or otherwise circulated, in any form of binding without the written permission of the publisher

British Library Cataloguing-in-Publication Data

A catalogue record for this book is available on request from the British Library

This book reproduces the text of the original edition. The content and language, reflect the beliefs, practices and terminology of their time, and have not been updated.

THE MOTHER'S COLUMN ABOUT FOOD.

IT is to be questioned whether of all the many topics that arouse men's passions or appeal to men's interests any transcends in importance that which relates to food. It was so when the world was young and gay; it will be so when the world is a good deal greyer and older than it is now. "Our little systems have their day," as Tennyson writes: but the food question remains ever the same—the first on men's lips, the nearest and dearest to men's hearts. Indeed, it may be said that as man becomes more civilised he takes more interest in the subject than ever. "Animals feed," says Savarin, "man eats; the man of intellect alone knows how to eat." Equally true is another of Savarin's profound aphorisms. "The fate of nations depends upon how they are fed." In our day the question of prepared food is increasingly important. It did not much matter in the primitive simplicity of the Garden of Eden, where Adam and Eve lived happily on fruit, which was ripe and ready once a week and all the year round. Then cookery was an unknown art. Alas! since the Fall such are necessities of the case, it is the art of arts, the science of sciences, the blessing of blessings, the crowning glory of refinement of knowledge and civilisation. A man's happiness mainly depends upon the state of his stomach, and that is a blessing or a curse, as cookery is rightly understood. A man who cannot digest his food, whose stomach is out of order, is a source of annoyance to himself and all around. They who cannot get their daily bread are apt to be dangerous. But in modern times, and especially in a country like England, with its ports open to receive its food supplies from every quarter of the world, the great topic of the time is not so much where to procure one's food as how to cook it. Farinaceous food is the staff of life, but even that may be prepared in such a way as to render it difficult of digestion and the cause of many evils. It may safely be affirmed that a great deal of the illness in the metropolis for instance, is occasioned by the way in which adulterated flour is prepared for household consumption. Infant mortality may be safely affirmed to have thus received an enormous increase. In Paris, as was to be expected, our lively and clever neighbours, perceiving this to be the case, were not long in profiting by this state of things, and in producing prepared food, which was at once to save the life of the infant and to give renewed vigour and zest to the confirmed invalid. So sedulously were all these preparations put forth that the French Government instituted an inquiry as to the nature of their contents. It was discovered that they were very simple preparations; but, nevertheless, the idea of prepared food became more popular than ever. Scientific men took up the subject; and in our own country a medical man of the name of Ridge especially distinguished himself in this way. Originally he had no other idea than that of providing the best form of food possible for infants and invalids. It was cooked a gallon or so at the time, and was given away by the Doctor to his patients and friends. By degrees the demand became too large for gratuitous distribution. Nor can this be wondered at, since it vies with milk in containing all the necessary elements for the support of vigorous life, and is much more easily procured. As, alas! pure, good milk is one of the things yet difficult to be discovered in poor neighbourhoods, in our great cities especially, some nourishing substitute was required. The next thing was to patent Dr. Ridge's Cooked Food and prepare it on an extensive scale. Hence the establishment of the large manufactory at Kingsland portrayed in our present number. From this manufactory thousands of tins and packets are daily sent out to the public. There it is prepared on the largest scale for an ever-increasing market. Nor are we surprised to learn that this is the case, as every mother who uses it praises it. The Food can be got ready for use in one minute's boiling, a fact which renders Dr. Ridge's Patent Cooked Food especially valuable and especially superior to all other preparations of the kind. Time is money, it is often said. Where invalids and infants are concerned it means more—it is life itself. —*Penny Illustrated Paper, December 1, 1877.*

Dr. Ridge's PATENT COOKED Food
FOR INFANTS, INVALIDS, &c

SWINBORNE'S
PATENT REFINED ISINGLASS,
EXTRA QUALITY,

In 1/- Packets—and Patent Isinglass in 8d. Packets—is specially recommended for INVALIDS and INFANTS.

A little should be taken in Tea, Milk, or Broth.

SWINBORNE'S
PATENT CALVES' FEET GELATINE,

In 6d. and 1/- Packets, is the cheapest and best for making Jellies, Blanc Manges, &c.

D. BUMSTED & CO.

By Special Appointment TO Her Majesty the Queen.

Prize Medals, Paris and London.

SALT.

Royal British Table Salt

IN JARS, BOTTLES, AND PACKETS.

A SUPPLEMENT TO ALL COOKERY BOOKS.
New Edition, Price 1s., Revised and Enlarged.

ECONOMICAL COOKERY

FOR THE MIDDLE CLASSES.   By MRS. ADDISON.

Containing 300 Recipes for Soups, Fish, Meats, Vegetables, Puddings, and Sweets.

QUEEN.—"Full of really economical recipes. Some are taken from foreign cookery, and nearly all of them have something novel about them."
OXFORD JOURNAL.—"Dainty dishes, both novel and inexpensive."

IMPROVED EDITION, 396 pages, Price 2s. 6d., cloth.

THE DOMESTIC WORLD.

A PRACTICAL GUIDE IN ALL THE DAILY DIFFICULTIES OF DOMESTIC AND SOCIAL ECONOMY.

BY THE AUTHOR OF "ENQUIRE WITHIN."

COURT JOURNAL.—"The subjects are arranged in alphabetical order, so that a reference to any of them is an easy matter. The book is of the highest utility."
BRADFORD CHRONICLE.—"This most useful and instructive book."
OXFORD CHRONICLE.—"Almost every subject connected with home and domestic life is treated in a thoroughly practical manner, and in clear and simple language."
BRISTOL MERCURY.—"Crammed with useful information, and deserves to be as popular as the author's previous work."
SHEFFIELD POST.—"The book is in every respect a perfect treasure."
LEICESTER CHRONICLE.—"We are surprised at the abundance and variety of the matter on which it speaks."

LONDON: HODDER & STOUGHTON PATERNOSTER ROW.

TRADE **ELECTRICITY IS LIFE** MARK.

PULVERMACHER'S IMPROVED PATENT
GALVANIC CHAIN BANDS, BELTS, BATTERIES, &c.

Approved by the Academy of Medicine of Paris, and other Medical Authorities in England and Abroad.

THESE HIGHLY-IMPROVED INVENTIONS render electricity, in a mild continuous form, perfectly self-applicable and extremely efficacious, no shock or unpleasant sensation being experienced, thus it becomes a true fountain of health and vigour, speedily soothing agonising pains, reanimating torpid limbs, reviving the sluggish functions of life, and imparting renewed energy and vitality to constitutions enfeebled by various influences.

THE DAILY INCREASING NUMBER OF CURES EFFECTED BY

PULVERMACHER'S MEDICO-GALVANIC SYSTEM
IN CASES OF

Indigestion,	**Loss of Voice,**	**Rheumatism,**
Liver Complaints,	**Asthma,**	**Constipation,**
Neuralgia,	**Bronchitis,**	**General Debility,**
Sciatica,	**Paralysis,**	**Female Complaints,**
Deafness,	**Epilepsy,**	**Functional Disorders, &c.,**

is proved by innumerable Testimonials both Medical and Private. These GALVANIC CHAIN BANDS, by supplying the electrical deficiency, constitute Nature's most congenial curative in the ailments referred to, thereby embodying a host of remedies in one.

Thirty-five years' successful experience has proved the marvellous remedial powers of these appliances, even in cases defying ordinary treatment.

Mr. PULVERMACHER refrains from advancing statements of his own in favour of his MEDICO-GALVANIC APPLIANCES, but confines himself mainly to quotations from the opinions of competent medical and scientific authorities, including Sir C. LOCOCK, Bart, M.D., F.R.C.S.; Sir HENRY HOLLAND, Bart., M.D., F.R.C.S., and F.R.S.; Sir J. R. MARTIN, Bart., C.B., F.R.C.S., F.S.A., and F.R.S.; Sir W. FERGUSSON, Bart., M.D., F.R.S., F.R.C.S. See Pamphlet, "GALVANISM, NATURE'S CHIEF RESTORER OF IMPAIRED VITAL ENERGY," sent free on application to

MR. J. L. PULVERMACHER, GALVANIC ESTABLISHMENT
194 REGENT STREET, LONDON, W.
(Nearly opposite Conduit Street.)

TASTY DISHES.

BROWN & POLSON'S CORN FLOUR.

BROWN and POLSON have the satisfaction of republishing, by special permission, the following Instructions issued by

THE NATIONAL TRAINING SCHOOL FOR COOKERY,

which are a further recognition of the merits of a manufacture which BROWN and POLSON were the first to initiate, and which they have carried to an unrivalled perfection.

A valuable HANDBOOK OF COOKERY (published by Messrs. Chapman and Hall) contains the following amongst other lessons:—

PUDDINGS.

Lesson No. 15.—Corn Flour Pudding.

Average cost of a "Corn Flour Pudding" (in a cup).

INGREDIENTS.

	d.
2 dessert-spoonsful of corn flour...	1
¼ pint of milk ...	1
6 lumps of sugar ...	0¼
1 egg ...	1
Time required, about an hour.	3¼

Now we will show you how to make a Corn Flour Pudding (in a cup, for infants or invalids).

1. We put a saucepan half full of warm water on the fire to boil.
2. We put two dessert-spoonsful of corn flour into the saucepan.
3. We pour in by degrees half a pint of milk, mixing it very smoothly. N.B.—We must be careful that it does not get lumpy.
4. We now add to it six lumps of sugar, put the saucepan on the fire, and stir smoothly until it boils; it will take about ten minutes.
5. We then move the saucepan to the side of the fire.
6. We break one egg into the saucepan, and beat it up until it is all well mixed.
7. We take a cup (just large enough to hold the pudding), and grease it inside with a piece of butter.
8. We pour the mixture out of the saucepan into the cup.
9. We take a small cloth, wring it out in boiling water, flour it well, and tie it over the top of the cup with a piece of string. N.B.—We should tie the four corners of the cloth over the top of the cup.
10. When the water in the saucepan is quite boiling, we put it in the cup and let it boil for twenty-five minutes.
11. For serving, we take the cloth off the cup, and the pudding may be turned out or not, according to taste.

CAKES.

Lesson No. 6.—Corn Flour Cake.

Average cost of a "Corn Flour Cake" (about three-quarters of a pound).

INGREDIENTS.

	d.
¼ lb. of corn flour ...	2
2 oz. of butter ...	2
¼ lb. of loaf sugar ...	1
1 teaspoonful of baking powder ...	0½
2 eggs ...	2
	7¼

Time required, about an hour.

Now we will show you how to make Corn Flour Cake.

1. We put two ounces of butter into a basin, and beat it to a cream.
2. We add to the butter a quarter of a pound of pounded loaf sugar and mix it well.
3. We break in two eggs and beat all well together.
4. We now stir lightly into the mixture a quarter of a pound of Corn Flour and a teaspoonful of baking powder, and beat it well together for five minutes.
5. We grease a cake-tin inside with butter or dripping.
6. We pour the mixture into the tin and put it immediately into the oven (the heat should rise to 240 deg.) to bake for half-an-hour.
7. After that time we turn the cake out of the tin and slant it against a plate until it is cold. (This will prevent it getting heavy.) N.B.—If preferred, the mixture could be baked in small tins instead of one large one, in which case it would only take fifteen minutes to bake.

BROWN & POLSON'S CORN FLOUR.

(ALL RIGHTS RESERVED.)

TASTY DISHES;

MADE FROM TESTED RECIPES.

SHOWING

WHAT WE CAN HAVE

FOR

BREAKFAST, DINNER, TEA, AND SUPPER.

ONE HUNDRED AND TWENTIETH THOUSAND.

WITH APPENDIX CONTAINING ADDITIONAL RECIPES.

London:
JAMES CLARKE & CO., 13 & 14, FLEET STREET.

1897.

Used exclusively in the HOTEL CECIL, a number of the Gordon Hotels, and other principal Hotels and Restaurants.

VICTORIA DATE VINEGAR

DELICIOUS in flavour and aroma, and pronounced by experts in culinary matters SUPERIOR to Wine or Malt Vinegars.

SOLD EVERYWHERE.

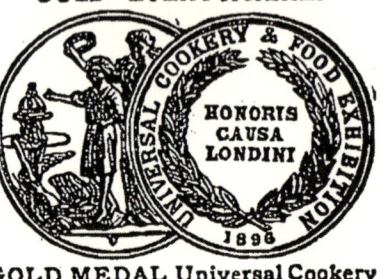

FOR TABLE USE.

Best for **PICKLING AND ALL** Domestic Purposes.

Try "DERBY" SAUCE, piquant, delicious, prepared in Victoria Date Vinegar.

A Tasting Sample of the Vinegar will be sent Post Free on receipt of application to

THE VICTORIA DATE CO., LTD., Victoria Works, 112, Belvedere Rd., Lambeth, S.E.

GOLD MEDAL Universal Cookery and Food Exhibition, 1896.

UNIVERSAL COOKERY & FOOD EXHIBITION — HONORIS CAUSA LONDINI — 1896

BRILLIANT WHITE SILENT LIGHT.

WILLIAM SUGG'S

CELEBRATED PATENT

GAS BURNERS.

WITH SELF-ACTING GOVERNORS.

PREVENTING WASTE AND FLARING.

See that all Burners and Glasses bear my Trade-Mark. To be obtained of all Gasfitters.

Coloured Illustrations and Prices on Application.

WILLIAM SUGG, Vincent Works, Vincent Street, Westminster, S.W.

Show Rooms—Exactly opposite Charing Cross Post Office.

PUBLISHERS' NOTE.

"What shall we have?" is a question daily asked in thousands of homes by troubled housekeepers, as often calling forth only the same ever-repeated answer. It is this perpetually-recurring query that has suggested the publication of the present book, as an attempt to furnish a ready answer of a more satisfactory nature. It is not a Cookery Book, in the ordinary sense of the term: making no profession of teaching how to cook, or even of embracing a very wide range of recipes. It pretends to be simply what its title describes—a selection of fresh and choice recipes for Tasty Dishes; nearly every one of which has been personally tested by the compiler.

The volume is published with the hope that it may, by suggesting a pleasing variety of simple palatable dishes, be the means of lifting a burden from many a housewife's heart, and increasing in some degree the general peace and comfort of many a household. The Publishers believe that it will be warmly welcomed as affording opportunity of enjoying variety without vexation; and they have full confidence that the recipes will commend themselves in all homes where it is desired to have excellence without extravagance.

INDISPENSABLE TO EVERY HOME.

Useful alike in Palace, Mansion, or Cottage.

NYE'S IMPROVED PATENT COMBINED
MINCING & SAUSAGE MACHINES

Are indispensable for preparing an immense variety of "Tasty Dishes." They are beautifully finished, last a life-time, and are up-to-date in every respect. **Prices 8/6, 10/6, 12/6, 16/-, 21/-, 30/-, 42/-, 63/-, carriage paid.**

For other patterns see Illustrated Catalogue.

Nye's are the original patents.

Beware of inferior imitations with Poisonous LEAD interior fittings. Demand Nye's and refuse all others, or order direct from the Makers.

NYE'S PATENT MILLS
for Coffee, Pepper, &c.

The only way to be absolutely certain of getting *genuine* and *freshly-ground* Coffee, &c., is to grind it at home as required. These Mills are handy, quick-grinding, and very durable, the grinding surfaces being hardened by a peculiar process. They are arranged to clamp on table or screw to wall, as preferred. **Prices 4/6, 6/-, 8/-, 10/-, 14/-, carriage paid.**

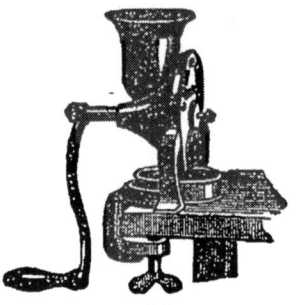

TABLE MILL.

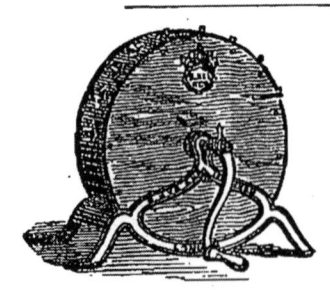

NYE'S IMPROVED
KNIFE CLEANING MACHINES.

The best quality that can be made. As supplied under special contract to H.M. Government. From 21/- to £12 10s., according to size, carriage paid to any railway station in the kingdom.

Machines of all Makers repaired as New. Estimates free.

THE GENUINE MACHINES HAVE NYE'S NAME CAST ON THEM.

Illustrated Catalogue of NYE'S Inventions sent free on application.

NYE'S, Berwick House, Oxford Street
(Opposite Wells Street), LONDON, W.

CONTENTS.

SOUPS.

	PAGE		PAGE
Baked Soup	2	Lentil Soup	7
Beef ,,	3	Mutton ,,	4
Carrot ,,	4	Oxtail ,,	8
General Directions for Soup making	1	Palestine Soup	9
Graham ,,	5	Potatoe ,,	9
Green Pea Soup	4	Sheep's Head Soup	10
Haricot Bean ,,	6	Tomato ,,	11
Jugged ,,	6	Tomatoes, Purée of	12

FISH.

	PAGE		PAGE
Cod, Baked	14	Oysters, Curried	14
,, Cutlets	15	Salmon Cutlets	15
,, ,, à la Reine	16	,, ,, à la Reine	16
,, Salt, with Egg Sauce	16	,, ,, Baked	23
Eels, Stewed, à l'Americain	17	,, ,, en Papillotte	24
Fish Balls	18	,, ,, of cold Fish No. 1	25
,, Croquettes	19	,, ,, ,, No. 2	26
,, Fritters	19	,, Moulded	22
,, Mayonnaise	22	,, Potted	25
,, Pâtés	20	Soles, Filleted (white)	13
,, Pie	21		

MEAT AND POULTRY.

	PAGE		PAGE
Beef Cakes	31	Kidneys, Stewed	45
,, Browned Mince of	31	,, à la Brochette	46
,, Breakfast Dish of	32	Lamb, Stewed Breast of	33
,, Croquettes	32	,, Minced with Poached Eggs	33
,, Rump Steak, Rolled No. 1	27	Mock Pigeons	53
,, ,, ,, No. 2	28	Mutton Cutlets, No. 1	47
,, ,, ,, Stewed No. 1	28	,, ,, No. 2	47
,, ,, ,, No. 2	29	,, Baked Breast of	48
,, ,, ,, Broiled	30	,, à la Jardinière	48
Camp Pie	42	Rabbit Pie	36
Chicken, Bondinettes of	34	,, Jugged	37
,, Potted	39	,, Boudinettes of	34
,, Pâtés	39	Tongue, Jellied	52
,, Minced, and Eggs	40	Turkey, Pulled	34
Curries	41	,, Scallop	32
,, Rice for	42	Veal Pâtés	53
Devilled Meat	43	,, Jellied	52
Old Fowl, To Cook an	38	,, Scallop	52
Kidneys Fried	43	,, Bondinettes of	34
,, Toasted	44	,, Cutlets, Stewed	53
,, Broiled	45	,, Cake	54

CONTENTS.

PUDDINGS AND SWEETS.

	PAGE		PAGE
Agra Pudding	61	Lemon Puddings	81
Apple Méringue	57	,, Méringue	82
,, Pudding Baked	58	,, Trifle	82
,, ,, Swiss	60	Marmalade Pudding, boiled	83
,, Charlotte	58	,, ,, baked	83
,, Soufflé	59	,, Custard Pudding	84
,, Fritters	60	Mysterious Pudding	84
Arrowroot Charlotte	61	Newark	85
,, Creams	62	Orange Fritters	86
Austrian Pudding	62	,, Pudding	86
Bachelor's ,,	64	,, Méringue, see Lemon	82
Betsy ,,	64	,, Jelly	87
Bread Fritters	63	Paste, Puff	55
,, and Butter Pudding, Boiled	63	Pastry, Short, No. 1	56
Carrot Pudding	64	,, ,, No. 2	57
Cherry Bread Pudding	68	Pearl Barley Pudding, No. 1	87
Christmas Pudding, No. 1	65	,, ,, No. 2	88
,, ,, No. 2	65	Queen of Puddings	88
,, ,, No. 3 (Impromptu)	66	,, ,, with Strawberry	
Citron Pudding	66	,, Méringue	89
Claret Jelly	71	Queen's Toast	90
Coconut Pudding	71	Rhenish Cream	95
Cornflour Hasty Pudding	68	Rhubarb Fritters	90
,, Méringue	69	,, Jelly	91
Cream Raspberry Pie	67	,, Fool	91
Currant Fritters	72	,, Méringue Tarts	92
Curate Pudding	70	,, ,, Pie	92
Delhi Pudding	72	Rice, Moulded	93
Egg Jelly	73	,, Ground, Pudding, Boiled	93
Fig Pudding, No. 1	74	,, Méringue	94
,, ,, No. 2	74	,, Cheesecakes	94
,, Custard	74	,, Flummery	95
Floating Island	75	St. Thomas' Pudding	99
French Pancakes	73	Snow Pudding	96
General Satisfaction	76	,, Drift Pudding	97
German Puffs	77	Solid Custard	96
Gingerbread Pudding	77	Sponge-cake Pudding	98
Gooseberry Pudding, Baked	78	,, Custard	98
,, Fool	78	Strawberry Méringue	97
,, rich	79	Tea-cup Plum Pudding	100
Half-Pay Pudding	79	Third Buffs	100
Kentish Pudding Pies	80	Uncle Toby's ,,	101
Lemon Pie	80	Welcome Guest ,,	101
,, Creams	81		

CAKES.

	PAGE		PAGE
A Plain Cake	103	Rice Buns	109
Biscuits	103	Rusks	109
Christmas Cake	104	Scotch Shortbread	111
Gingerbread Loaf	104	Scones	114
,, Whole wheat meal	104	Seed Cake	113
,, Cakes, plain	105	Sly Cakes	113
Lunch Cake	105	Soda Cake	110
Madeira ,,	106	,, Buns	110
Orange ,,	106	Sponge Cakes	112
Oswego ,,	107	Tea Cakes, No. 1	114
Pound ,,	107	,, ,, No. 2	114
Queen's Buns	108	Victoria Buns	115
Rice Cakes	108	White Cake	116
,, Cake	109	Yorkshire Cake	116

CONTENTS.

EGGS.

	PAGE
Eggs sur le Plat	117
,, Toasted	117
,, Baked No. 1	118
,, ,, No. 2	119
,, Fricasseed	119
,, Cutlets	120
Eggs Potted	121
,, Stirred	121
,, Scalloped	122
,, Whirled	122
,, Poached with Mushrooms	123

ODDS AND ENDS.

	PAGE
Apples Fried	130
Apple Jelly	139
Baking Powder	130
Celery Stewed	131
,, Salad	131
,, Baked	132
,, Sauce	132
Cheese Fingers	125
,, Biscuits	125
,, Pâtés	126
,, Fondu	127
,, Sandwiches	127
Crusts, Four ways of Using	129
Cucumbers Fried	130
Horseradish Sauce	128
Ladies' Cabbage	136
Lemon Syrup	128
,, Conserve	141
Macaroni with Tomato Sauce	136
Mincemeat	140
Orange Marmalade	142
Parsnip Fritters	135
Potatoes Whipped	133
Potato Puff	133
,, Cakes	134
,, Scallops	134
,, Chips	135
,, Balls	135
Preserved Ginger—Imitation	140
Rhubarb Jam, Green	143
,, ,, Red	144
Ripe Gooseberry Jam	142
Spinach with Egg Dressing	137
,, ,, Poached Eggs	138
Tomato Salad	138
Tomatoes Baked	139

ADDITIONAL RECIPES.

SOUPS—
Onion Soup	145
Potatoe ,,	146
Rabbit ,,	146
Vegetable Purée	147

FISH AND MEAT—
American Fritters	149
Beef Olives	151
Boiled Brains	150
Canapées of Sardines	148
Roulades of Beef	150
Sardines on Toast	148
Soles in Batter	149
Stewed Steak and Macaroni	152
Swiss Pâtés	153
Veal Shape	152

PUDDINGS AND SWEETS—
Alpine Pudding	154
Apple Batter Pudding	154
,, Custard	155

PUDDINGS & SWEETS—continued.
Apple Puff	157
,, Snow No. 1	155
,, ,, No. 2	154
Bachelor's Pudding No. 2	157
Cup Puddings	158
Custards	163
Fig Pudding No. 3	158
Free Kirk Pudding	154
German Pancakes	160
Gingerbread Cup Pudding	159
Gooseberry Jelly	163
Jam Puff	160
Lemon Cheesecakes	162
Sir Watkin Wynne Pudding	161
Thorpe Pudding	161
Wafer ,,	162

ODDS AND ENDS—
Dinner for an Invalid	164
Frosted Vegetables	166
Recipe for Making Coffee	165

ARTICLES ON Cookery Recipes, Kitchen Ranges, Domestic Matters, Dress & Fashion, Fancy Work, &c.,

ARE GIVEN IN

The Bazaar, Exchange & Mart,

AND JOURNAL OF THE HOUSEHOLD,

Which is published every Monday, Wednesday, and Friday
Price 2d., by post 2½d.
Specimen Copy, Two Penny Stamps.

ADVERTISEMENTS of or for Domestic Appliances, Furniture, Sewing Machines, Dress Materials, And Other Property,

ONE PENNY FOR THREE WORDS.

"The Bazaar" Office, 170, Strand, London, W.C.

TASTY DISHES.

SOUPS.

General Directions for Soupmaking.

Lean beef, mutton, or veal, is the basis of all good rich soups, but fresh bones and those from cooked meat and poultry, with trimmings of meat, make very good stock where economy is desired. The meat should be cut up very small and the bones well cracked, and simmered from three to six hours, or longer, according to the quantity. As a rule, a quart of water may be allowed to each pound of meat for soup. Let it heat gradually and remove the scum as it rises, taking care that it does not *boil*. When it is well skimmed, add the vegetables, which may be one or two turnips carrots, parsnips, and an onion with a few cloves stuck into it, and a small bunch of sweet herbs. When finished, turn it into stockpot or pan, and set it aside till morning, when the fat can be easily removed. The stock should then be strained through a fine wire sieve or coarse cloth, and it is ready for use. Do not add salt till the meat is thoroughly cooked.

Most soups are as good on the second day as when first sent to table, unless they are warmed up too quickly or left upon the fire too long after they are hot; in the one case they are apt to scorch, and in the other they become insipid. When any is left from a meal it should be allowed to get cool without covering it.

In all the following recipes for soup any of the vegetables mentioned may be omitted if the stock has been already flavoured with them.

Baked Soup.

Ingredients.—2 lbs. lean beef, 1 head of celery, 2 turnips, 1 teacup of chopped cabbage, 1 onion, 1 carrot, chopped parsley, 4 or 6 tomatoes (or ½ tin of preserved tomatoes), ½ a cup of rice previously boiled for 15 minutes, pepper and salt, 5 pints of cold water.

Method.—Cut the meat into dice, peel and chop up all the vegetables, add the rice and seasoning, mix all well together, and put into a strong earthenware jar, pour in the water, fit the cover on closely, and set in the oven in a pan of boiling water for 6 hours. Do not uncover it while it is cooking, and serve without further preparation.

Note.—This is a very substantial winter soup.

Beef Soup.

Ingredients.—¾ lb. of lean beef, ¼ lb. of rice, ¼ lb. each of turnip, carrot, and tomatoes, 3 stalks of celery, *or* 3 sprigs of parsley.

Method.—Cut the meat into pieces about ½ an inch square; wash and pick over the rice; peel and cut into ½-inch squares the turnip, carrot, and tomatoes; cut the celery or parsley very small. Put the meat in a soup-kettle with four quarts of cold water, and bring it slowly to a boil; then add the vegetables, prepared as above, a level tablespoonful of salt, and a quarter of a saltspoonful of pepper, and boil the soup gently until all its ingredients are tender. By the addition of boiling water increase the soup when it is done to its original quantity of four quarts; see that it is properly seasoned, and serve it hot.

Mutton Soup.

Use the above directions, substituting mutton for beef, pearl barley for rice, and onions for tomatoes. Do not skim either of the above-named soups.

Note.—These soups are made in the New York Cookery Schools, and are considered very nutritious.

Carrot Soup.

Ingredients.—To each quart of stock allow 12 or 13 ozs. of pulped carrot, salt and cayenne to taste.

Method.—Boil as many carrots as required (about 4 good-sized ones to each quart) till quite tender. Then cut up the *red* part and rub it through a sieve. Weigh it and add gravy soup or good stock in the above proportions; mix it gradually and season with salt and a little cayenne. Let it boil up, and serve very hot, with a dish of fried bread cut into small dice.

Green Pea Soup.

Ingredients.—2 quarts of stock, ½ peck of old peas, 2 lettuce, 1 onion, a few sprigs of mint, and a little cucumber, 1 tablespoonful of butter, 1 tablespoonful of flour.

Method.—Reserve 1 quart of stock and a teacupful of peas; put the rest of stock and all the vegetables together and simmer till quite tender, then press all through a sieve; add the remainder of the stock, let it come to the boiling point, and just before serving, if the soup is not very thick add the butter and flour well mixed together. Boil the teacup of peas by themselves, put them in the tureen and pour the soup over them. Serve with a dish of toasted bread.

Graham Soup.
(VEGETABLES ONLY.)

Ingredients.—3 onions, 3 carrots, 4 turnips, 1 small cabbage, 1 head of celery, 1 pint of stewed tomatoes (tinned will do), a small bunch of sweet herbs, 1 tablespoonful of butter, ½ a cup of milk, thickened with cornflour, pepper and salt, 3 quarts of water.

Method.—Chop all the vegetables, except the cabbage and tomatoes, very fine, and set them over the fire with rather over 3 quarts of water. Simmer gently for half-an-hour, at the end of which time the cabbage must be added, having previously been parboiled and chopped up. In fifteen minutes more put in the tomatoes and a bunch of sweet herbs, and give all a good boil for twenty minutes longer. Put through a colander; return the soup to the fire; stir in a good tablespoonful of butter, pepper, and salt, ½ a cup of milk, thickened with cornflour; let it boil up, and it is ready for the table.

Note.—This is a good thick, palatable soup, and is more quickly made than those in which meat is used.

Haricot Bean Soup.

Ingredients.—2 quarts of stock, 1 pint of haricot beans, pepper and salt to taste.

Method.—Soak the beans all night in cold water, drain them and boil in cold water, slightly salted, till quite tender, about one and a-half hours. Press them through a sieve with a spoon, and add them (leaving out the husks) to the stock, which should be warm; add pepper and salt to taste, boil up once more, and serve with a dish of fried bread cut into small dice.

Jugged Soup.

Ingredients.—2 quarts of stock—it need not be *very* good, 5 or 6 slices of streaked pork cut very thin, 6 parboiled potatoes, 1 sliced onion, 6 sliced tomatoes, 1 carrot grated, 1 cupful of green peas, ¼ teacup of raw rice, salt and pepper, a few bits of butter, a few sweet herbs finely chopped.

Method.—Lay in a strong stoneware jar, some slices of parboiled potatoes, and on these 2 or 3 thin slices of pork, then the vegetables and rice in alternate layers, and sprinkle a little pepper, salt, and minced herbs over each layer. Then put more pork, rice, and vegetables alternately till all are used up. Pour the stock over this, fit on the lid, and cover with a paste of flour and water to exclude the air; set in a pan of boiling water and place in a moderate oven for 4 hours at least. Serve in a tureen without further preparation.

Lentil Soup.

Ingredients.—4 carrots, 2 sliced onions, 1 cut lettuce, 2 ozs. butter, 2 pints lentils, the crumbs of 2 French rolls, 2 quarts of medium stock.

Method.—Put the vegetables, with the butter, into a stewpan, and let them simmer for five minutes; then add the lentils, which should be soaked in cold water for two hours previously, and 1 pint of the stock, and stew gently for half-an-hour. Now fill up with the remainder of the stock, let it boil another hour, and put in the crumbs of the rolls. When these are well soaked, rub all through a wire sieve or tammy cloth. Season to taste with pepper and salt, boil up once more, and serve.

Water may be used in the place of the stock, if desired; but in that case a cup of milk, thickened with cornflour, should be added just before the final boil.

Oxtail Soup.

Ingredients.—2 quarts of stock, made from fresh bones, 1 oxtail, 2 carrots, 1 onion, a little thyme and parsley, pepper and salt, 2 tablespoonfuls of browned flour, and 1 tablespoonful of ketchup.

Method.—Cut the tail into joints, and fry in good dripping; cut the vegetables into slices, and add them, with the herbs, to the stock—which should have been skimmed and strained—put in the tail, and simmer gently for four hours. Remove the pieces of tail carefully, strain the soup, add pepper and salt to the taste, and a tablespoonful of ketchup, and thicken with a tablespoonful of baked flour wet with cold water. Put back the pieces of tail, simmer gently for five or ten minutes, and serve. If the stock has been already flavoured with vegetables, those mentioned above may be omitted, or a few slices of carrot only may be served in the soup. Stock should *always* be prepared the day before the soup is required. A very simple method of making oxtail soup is to add the contents of a pint tin of prepared oxtail soup to 3 pints of stock.

Potato Soup.

Ingredients.—3 pints of white stock (from mutton or veal), 3 lbs. of good mealy potatoes, 3 onions, yolks of 2 eggs, ½ a pint of milk, pepper and salt to taste.

Method.—Strain the stock, and put it over the fire to heat. In the meantime peel 3 lbs. of good mealy potatoes and 3 onions, season with pepper and salt, and boil till quite tender. When done, press them through a sieve, and add them to the boiling stock. Just before serving add the yolks of 2 eggs, beaten into ½ a pint of milk. This must be done gradually, and the soup must on no account be allowed to boil after these are added. Send to table quite hot, with a dish of fried bread, cut into dice.

Palestine Soup.

Ingredients.—3 lbs. of Jerusalem artichokes, 3 turnips, 1 head of celery, 1 onion, 1 lump of sugar, salt and cayenne to taste, and sufficient white stock (from mutton or veal) to cover them.

Method.—Put these all together into a stewpan, and boil gently for an hour, or until the vegetables are quite tender; then rub them through a sieve put back into the stewpan, and boil up once more. Just before serving add ½ a pint of milk or cream —a little more if the soup is very thick—but after this is added it must not be allowed to *boil* again. Send to table with a dish of fried bread cut into very small dice. This is an excellent white table soup.

Note.—If preferred, the artichokes may be boiled separately in water, then pressed through the sieve, and added to the stock. This method saves any waste of the soup.

Sheep's Head Soup.

Ingredients.—1 sheep's head, 4 quarts of cold water, 2 turnips, 2 carrots, 2 heads of celery, a bunch of sweet herbs, 1 onion, a cup of milk thickened with cornflour. *For the Forcemeat Balls:* The tongue and brains, with an equal quantity of fine breadcrumbs, pepper and salt to taste, a little minced parsley, 1 egg.

Method.—Get the butcher to clean and prepare the head as he would a calf's head for soup, with the skin on, and split it so that the tongue and brains can be taken out. Break the bone of the head, wash it well in several waters and lay in salted water for half-an-hour; cover with fresh water and heat

SOUPS.

gradually to a boil, then drain off all the water, so as to remove any peculiar odour. Now cover it with 4 quarts of cold water, and put in all the vegetables, which should be chopped small, simmer from 4 to 6 hours, and strain into a basin, pressing all the nourishment out of the meat, then let it stand till cold so that the fat can be removed. Press the vegetables through a colander and reserve them till the fat has been taken from the soup. Meanwhile the tongue and brains should have been boiled separately and chopped up, then rubbed to a paste together, mixed with the bread crumbs, pepper, salt, and parsley, bound with the beaten egg, and rolled into small balls dipped in flour. Set these balls on a tin so that they do not touch each other, and place them in a quick oven till a crust is formed upon the top, then let them cool. Return the skimmed broth to the fire with the vegetables, boil up once, remove the scum and add the milk thickened with cornflour; simmer for 2 minutes after it boils, stirring all the time. Put the forcemeat balls in the tureen and pour the soup gently over, so as not to break them.

Note.—This soup should be made the day before it is wanted, it can then be heated, and the milk and forcemeat balls added just before serving.

Tomato Soup.

(VEGETABLES ONLY.)

Ingredients.—12 large red tomatoes, peeled and sliced, 1 small onion sliced, 2 tablespoonfuls of dripping, 1 tablespoonful of chopped parsley, pepper and salt, 1 teaspoonful of sugar, 1 small cup of boiled rice, 1 quart of boiling water, 1 tablespoonful of butter rolled in flour.

Method.—Put the onion and dripping into a stewpan, and simmer till of a reddish brown, add the tomatoes and stir all up till very hot, then pour upon them the boiling water and parsley; stew for half-an-hour and strain, rubbing the tomato through a sieve into the hot liquid. Return it to the stewpan, season with pepper, salt, and sugar, and when boiling again add the floured butter, and a minute later the rice; simmer ten minutes and serve.

Purée of Tomatoes.

Ingredients.—12 red tomatoes, 1 small minced onion, ½ pint of boiling water, 1 pint of boiling milk with ½ teaspoonful of soda stirred in, 2 tablespoonfuls of butter mixed with 1 tablespoonful of flour, 1 large teaspoonful of sugar, pepper and salt, 1 teacup of dry breadcrumbs.

Method.—Put the sliced tomatoes and onion over

the fire with the water and boil for half-an-hour, then strain and rub through a colander, working the tomatoes to a pulp. Meanwhile, boil the milk and soda, stir in the butter and flour, and after one boil, keep hot. Put the pepper, salt, and sugar with the tomatoes, and simmer for five minutes, pour them into the tureen, stir in the crumbs, and one minute later the thickened milk. Serve at once. If the milk be cooked with the tomatoes it will be sure to curdle.

FISH.

Curried Oysters.

Ingredients.—2 doz. oysters, 1 onion, 1 tablepoonful of curry-powder, 1 dessert-spoonful of flour, 2 ozs. butter, juice of a lemon.

Method.—Chop the onion up quite fine, mix the curry-powder, flour, and butter together, and put all these ingredients into a stewpan, and simmer till of a nice brown, stirring all the time; add the liquor of the oysters and the lemon-juice, and boil together for five minutes. Put in the oysters, boil up once, and serve with a dish of rice.

Baked Cod.

Ingredients.—The middle part of a large cod fish or a whole small one, a teacup of breadcrumbs, peppered and salted, 2 tablespoonfuls boiled salt pork, finely chopped, 1 tablespoonful of herbs—parsley, sweet marjoram, thyme, and a mere suspicion of minced onion—1 teaspoonful of anchovy or Harvey's sauce, ½ teacup of melted butter, juice of ½ a lemon, 1 beaten egg.

Method.—Lay the fish in cold, salted water for half-an-hour, then wipe it dry, and stuff it with a forcemeat, made of the crumbs, pork, herbs, onion and seasoning, bound with the beaten egg. Lay it in the baking-dish, and pour over it the melted butter. which should be quite thin, seasoned with the sauce, lemon-juice, pepper, and a pinch of parsley. Bake in a moderate oven for an hour, or longer, if the piece is large, basting frequently, lest it should brown too fast. Add a little butter and water if the sauce thickens too much. When the fish is done, remove it to a hot dish, strain the gravy over it, and serve. A few capers or chopped green pickles are considered a pleasant addition to the sauce.

Cutlets of Cod or Salmon.

Ingredients. — 3 lbs. fish cut in slices three-quarters-of-an-inch thick from the body of the fish, a handful of fine breadcrumbs, with which should be mixed pepper and salt, and a little minced parsley and 1 egg, beaten light. Enough butter, lard, or dripping to fry the cutlets.

Method.—Cut each slice of fish into strips, as wide as your two fingers, dry them with a clean cloth, rub lightly with salt and pepper, dip in the egg, then the breadcrumbs, and fry in enough fat to cover them well. Drain away every drop of fat, and lay upon hot white paper in a heated dish.

Cutlets of Cod or Salmon à la Reine.

Ingredients.—Prepare the fish as in the last recipe, until after frying it, when have ready the following sauce:—1 cup strong brown gravy (beef or veal), 1 teaspoonful anchovy sauce or mushroom ketchup, pepper, salt, a pinch of parsley, and a *very* little minced onion, 1 glass brown sherry and juice of half a lemon. Thicken with browned flour.

Method.—Lay the fried cutlets evenly on a broad saucepan with a lid, cover with the gravy and heat slowly all through, *but do not let them boil.* Take up the cutlets with care, and arrange upon a hot dish, and pour the gravy over them.

Note.—These are very nice, and well worth the additional trouble it may cost to prepare the sauce.

Salt Cod with Egg Sauce.

Ingredients.—1 lb. salt cod, previously soaked, then boiled and allowed to cool, picked or chopped fine; 1 small cup milk or cream, 1 teaspoonful corn-flour or flour, 2 eggs beaten light, 2 tablespoonfuls of butter, a little chopped parsley, half as much mashed potato as fish. Pepper to taste.

Method.—Heat the milk, thicken with the cornflour, then the potato rubbed very fine; next, the butter, the eggs, and parsley; lastly, the fish. Stir and toss until smoking hot all through, when pour into a deep dish.

Note.—Or, make a sauce of all the ingredients except the fish and potato. Mix these well together with a little melted butter, heat in a saucepan, stirring all the while; heap in the centre of a dish and pour the sauce over all.

Eels Stewed à l'Americain.

Ingredients.—3 lbs. eels, skinned and cleaned, and all the fat removed from the inside; 1 young onion, chopped fine; 4 tablespoonfuls of butter. Pepper and salt to taste, with chopped parsley.

Method.—Cut the eels in pieces, about two inches in length; season, and lay in a saucepan containing the melted butter. Strew the onion and parsley over all, cover the saucepan closely, and set in a pot of cold water. Bring this gradually to a boil, then cook very gently for an hour and a-half, or until the eels are tender. Turn out into a deep dish.

Filleted Soles (White).

Ingredients.—1 pair moderate-sized soles, lemon-juice, a little butter. *For the Sauce:* ½ oz. butter, ½ oz. flour, 1 tablespoonful of cream or milk, finely-chopped parsley.

Method.—Butter a plate, and lay on the fillets, which should be sprinkled with a few drops of lemon-juice; butter a piece of thin white paper, lay this over the fish, and put them into the oven for ten or fifteen minutes, according to size. Take them out, place them in the centre of a dish, and pour over "Maître d'Hôtel" sauce, made in the following manner:—½ ounce of butter, ½ oz. flour, stirred over a gentle heat, with a tablespoonful of cream or milk, and a little fish liquid—made from the bones and skin of the sole—and finely chopped parsley.

Fish Balls.

Ingredients.—Remains of any cold boiled fish—turbot, brill, or cod—potatoes, butter, a little milk.

Method.—Break the fish to pieces with a fork, removing every vestige of skin and bone, and shredding very fine. When this is done, add an equal bulk of mashed potatoes, work into a stiff batter, with a piece of butter and some milk, and, if you wish to have them very nice, a beaten egg. Flour your hands, and make the mixture into balls or ovates, and fry in boiling lard or dripping to a light brown.

Plainer fish cakes may be made of the cod and potatoes alone, moulded round like biscuits.

Fish Croquettes.

Ingredients.—Remains of cold fish—boiled, baked, or fried—one-third as much mashed potatoes, a little melted butter or white sauce, 1 beaten egg, chopped parsley, salt and pepper, seasoning of walnut ketchup or anchovy sauce.

Method.—Pick the fish carefully from the bones, and chop it fine; beat the potatoes to a cream with melted butter, add the parsley, pepper, salt, and sauce, and mix all well together. Make the mixture into balls or eggs, roll them in the beaten egg, strew over with fine breadcrumbs, and fry quickly in boiling fat. Serve very hot, with sliced lemon.

Fish Fritters.

Ingredients.—Remains of any cold boiled fish, about the same quantity of mashed potatoes, 1 small onion, pepper and salt, lard for frying, 1 egg.

Method.—Pick the fish from the bones and skin, and pound it in a mortar with the onion, season with pepper and salt, then well mix with it the mashed potatoes, and bind together with a well-beaten egg. Flatten the mixture out upon a dish or pastry board, cut into small rounds or squares and fry in boiling lard to a light brown. Pile it in a napkin on a very hot dish, garnish with parsley and serve with any kind of fish sauce.

Fish Pâtés.

Ingredients.—Pastry, remains of cold boiled salmon or cod, quarter as much mashed potato as fish, a little rich white sauce, pepper and salt to taste, a little parsley, yolks of one or two hard-boiled eggs—according to the number of pâtés—a spoonful of butter.

Method.—Roll out the pastry, which should be good and light, and cut into rounds about a quarter of an inch thick, and make twice as many as you wish to have pâtés. Lay half of them on a floured tin, with a small cutter take the centre part from the others, and lay the rings one on to each whole one, leaving a neat little round well in the middle; bake quickly, and glaze with beaten egg. *For filling:* Rub the sauce gradually into the mashed potato till both are free from lumps, and when mixed, beat to a cream; season and stir in the fish (which should be picked very fine), and in so doing *heap it up*, not beat it down. Do this quickly and lightly, fill the pastry shells, and set in the oven to heat through. Make a smooth paste with the yolk of the egg and butter, and when the pâtés are quite hot, spread a little over each; close the oven door for two minutes to set the paste, and serve.

Note.—Tinned lobster and salmon may be prepared in this manner. If the pâtés are well made, they form a very ornamental dish.

Fish Pie.

Ingredients.—Remains of cold boiled fish, 3 or 4 potatoes—boiled and mashed—a cup of melted butter, well seasoned with anchovy or other fish sauce, 1 teaspoonful of minced parsley, pepper and salt to taste.

Method.—Pull the pieces of fish apart with a fork, carefully removing all the bones, add to this the melted-butter sauce and parsley; when mixed, put it in a pie-dish, and cover with a layer of mashed potatoes, well seasoned with pepper and salt, and a small piece of butter. Cover the dish, and set in a moderate oven till it smokes and bubbles, then remove the cover, and brown before serving.

Mayonnaise of Fish.

Ingredients.—1 lb. or rather more of cold boiled fish, 3 hard-boiled eggs, 2 tablespoonfuls of best oil, 2 teaspoonfuls of sugar, 6 tablespoonfuls of vinegar 1 teaspoonful of salt, ½ teaspoonful each of pepper and made mustard, 2 heads of blanched lettuce.

Method.—Rub the yolks of the eggs smooth with the oil, add the sugar, salt, mustard, and pepper, and when these are well mixed, the vinegar, a few drops at a time. Set it by, covered, while you cut —not chop—the fish into strips about an inch long and shred the lettuce. Mix these in a salad bowl, pour over the dressing and garnish with rings of the whites of the eggs. Serve as soon as it is ready or the lettuce will become limp.

Note.—If preferred, the lettuce may be laid round the fish after the dressing is poured on, instead of being mixed with it.

Moulded Salmon.

Ingredients.—½ lb. of cold boiled salmon, 2 eggs beaten light, 2 tablespoonfuls of butter (melted, but not hot), 1 tablespoonful of fine breadcrumbs, seasoning of pepper, salt, and minced parsley.

Method.—Chop the fish fine, then rub it in a mortar or bowl with the back of a silver spoon, adding the butter until it is a smooth paste; beat the breadcrumbs into the eggs, and season before working all together. Put it into a buttered pudding-mould, and steam or boil for half-an-hour.

Sauce for the Above.—One cup of milk, heated to a boil and thickened with a tablespoonful of cornflour, 1 large spoonful of butter, 1 raw egg, 1 teaspoonful of anchovy, mushroom, or tomato ketchup, a small pinch of mace, and one of cayenne. Put the egg in last, and very carefully boil one minute to cook it, and when the pudding is turned from the mould, pour over it and serve. This is a nice supper dish, and tinned salmon may be used for it if liked, and the liquor added to the sauce.

Baked Salmon with Cream Sauce.

Ingredients.—A middle cut of salmon, 4 tablespoonfuls of butter, melted in hot water. *For the Sauce:* A cup of cream, 1 teaspoonful of cornflour, 1 tablespoonful of butter, pepper, salt, and parsley.

Method.—Butter a sheet of foolscap paper on both sides, and wrap the fish up in it, pinning the ends securely together. Lay in the baking pan, and pour six or seven spoonfuls of butter-and-water over it. Turn another pan over all, and steam in a moderate oven from three-quarters of an hour to an hour, lifting the cover from time to time to baste, and assure yourself that the paper is not burning. Meanwhile have ready in a saucepan a cup of cream, in which you would do well to dissolve a bit of soda a little larger than a pea. This is a wise precaution, whenever cream is to be boiled. Heat this in a vessel placed within another of hot water, thicken with a heaping teaspoonful of cornflour, add a tablespoonful of butter, pepper and salt to taste, a liberal pinch of minced parsley; and when the fish is unwrapped and dished pour half slowly over it, sending the rest to table in a boat.

Note.—If you have no cream use milk, and add a beaten egg to the thickening.

Salmon Cutlets en Papillote.

Ingredients.—Three or four slices of salmon, pepper and salt to taste.

Method.—Dry and lay in melted butter ten minutes. Dust lightly with cayenne pepper, and wrap securely in well buttered or oiled white paper, stitching down the ends of each cover. Fry in nice dripping or sweet lard. They will be done in ten minutes, unless very thick. Have ready clean, *hot* papers, fringed at both ends. Clip the thread of the soiled ones when you have drained them free from fat; slip dexterously and quickly, lest they cool in the process, into the fresh covers, give the fringed ends a twist, and send up on a heated dish. Salmon *en papillote* is also boiled by experts. If you attempt this be careful that the paper is so well greased and the cutlet turned so often that it does not scorch.

The least taste of burnt paper ruins the flavour of the fish, which it is the object of the covers to preserve.

Potted Salmon.

Ingredients.—¼ lb. of cold boiled salmon, 2 ozs. clarified butter, white pepper, cayenne, salt and mace to taste.

Method.—Pick the salmon from the bones, warm the butter, add the seasoning and pound all together in a mortar till it is of a smooth paste. Press into a glass jar and cover with clarified butter. This will keep good for several days in a cool place.

Salmon Cutlets.—No. 1.

Ingredients.—To every 6 ozs. of cold boiled salmon, add 2 ozs. mashed potatoes, white pepper, cayenne, salt and mace to taste, 1 egg, fine breadcrumbs.

Method.—See that the fish is perfectly free from bone, and pound it in a mortar, add the seasoning and potatoes, and form the mixture into the shape of small cutlets; brush each one over with beaten egg, sprinkle with crumbs and fry to a light brown. Serve quite plain for breakfast, but for dinner or supper send to table with anchovy sauce.

Salmon Cutlets.—No. 2.

Ingredients.—1 lb. cold boiled salmon, 2 eggs, white pepper, cayenne, salt and mace to taste, crumbs.

Method.—Pick the salmon from the bones, pound it with the seasoning, and mix together with the beaten eggs; form into cutlets, sprinkle with fine breadcrumbs and fry to a nice light brown. These cutlets are richer than those made from the above recipe, and can be served with or without anchovy sauce.

MEAT AND POULTRY.

Rolled Steak.—No. 1.

Ingredients.—Rump steak, forcemeat of breadcrumbs, pork, half an onion, pepper and salt; browned flour and butter for the gravy.

Method.—Take a good steak, not too thick, beat it flat with the broad side of a hatchet, and cover with a forcemeat made of breadcrumbs, a little minced pork, and half an onion. Moisten this slightly, and season to taste with salt and pepper. Roll the steak up, closely enclosing the stuffing, bind with twine into a compact bundle, and lay in a deep dish. Dash a teacupful of boiling water over it, cover with another dish, and bake about three-quarters of an hour, in its own steam. At the end of this time remove the cover, baste with a little butter, and dredge with flour to brown the meat. When it is a good colour, serve on a very hot dish. Thicken the gravy with a little browned flour and send it to table in a tureen. In removing the twine from the meat before serving, clip it in several places, that the form of the steak may not be disturbed.

Rolled Steak.—No. 2.

Ingredients.—Steak, 2 oz. breadcrumbs, parsley, a few sweet herbs, a very little butter, pepper and salt to taste.

Method.—Take a good rump steak, flatten it with a hatchet, and lay upon it a roll of seasoning made of the breadcrumbs, parsley, a few sweet herbs minced, pepper and salt, mixed with a little butter beaten to a cream with a fork. Roll up the steak, bind it evenly with fine twine, and lay it in a pie-dish with a cupful of boiling water. Cover with another dish, bake for forty minutes, basting frequently. Remove the cover and let it brown before sending to table. Thicken the gravy with a little browned flour, and serve very hot. A layer of oysters, bearded, instead of the forcemeat is a pleasant change. The twine should be cut off before sending to table.

Stewed Beef Steak.

Ingredients.—2 lbs. of beef steak cut 1½ inch thick, 1 carrot, 1 turnip, 1 onion, bunch of herbs, small piece of celery, 1 oz. of butter, ¾-pint of stock or water.

Method.—Cut off all the fat from the steak, and brown the meat in a saucepan in which 1 oz. of butter has been previously melted, turn with a spoon, not a fork. When the meat is brown on both sides pour off the fat, put in the vegetables cut up, and onion with brown skin left on, which gives colour to the gravy; roll 1 sprig of lemon thyme, 1 sprig common ditto, 1 sprig marjoram, 1 bay leaf or 2 sprigs of parsley, tie up, and add. Put on lid, simmer gently forty minutes in ¾-pint of cold stock or cold water. For thickening the gravy mix 1 oz. flour, a little salt and pepper, with a little water, and add ten minutes before serving; strain out the vegetables and serve fresh with it. Cut up the pieces of fat and cook separately on a tin plate in the oven; add to the dish of meat.

Stewed Rump Steaks.

Ingredients.—2 lbs. rump steak, 2 Spanish onions, 4 pickled walnuts, 3 carrots, 2 turnips, 1 tablespoonful of ketchup, 1 tablespoonful of flour, wet with 2 tablespoonfuls of water, pepper and salt, and rather more than 1 pint of water.

Method.—Choose rump steaks of tolerable thickness, and not too fat; divide them into pieces of convenient size, and fry them in a little butter, or clean beef-dripping, till of a nice brown on both sides. Have ready at the bottom of a stew-pan 2 onions peeled and chopped, 4 pickled walnuts cut up into bits, 3 carrots, and 2 turnips sliced and fried in the same fat as the beef was done in. Put all into a saucepan with rather more than a pint of water, and simmer gently for three hours; then skim well, and add one teaspoonful of salt, half that quantity of pepper, and a tablespoonful of ketchup, with a tablespoonful of flour and two of cold water, made as thickening, and let it boil up for a minute or so; it is then ready to serve. If stewed the day before it is wanted it is less rich, as the fat can be taken off; just thoroughly heating through is sufficient when required for table. If you please, you can omit the carrots and turnips, and throw in, ten minutes before serving, a dozen oysters, with their liquor strained through a sieve. Be careful not to let the stew boil for a moment after the oysters are added. Either way it is an extremely palatable dish; and properly done, ranks as an *entrée* or side-dish at dinner parties.

Broiled Steak.

Ingredients.—Rump steak, about an inch thick, butter, pepper, and salt.

Method.—Butter a sheet of white paper and twist the four corners so as to form a little tray, lay the steak in this and broil quickly from five to ten minutes, turning it once in the paper while cooking.

When done lay it on a hot dish, season with pepper and salt, add a little bit of butter, and serve at once.

Note.—Steak cooked in this way is much nicer than if broiled without the paper.

Beef Cakes.

Ingredients.—1 lb. of under-cooked roast beef, ¼ lb. of ham or bacon, a teaspoonful of sweet herbs, seasoning of pepper and salt, 1 large egg.

Method.—Mince the beef and ham, add herbs, &c., and mix with the egg, which must be previously well beaten, brush each cake over with a little white of egg; cover with bread crumbs, and fry quickly for five minutes.

Browned Mince of Beef.

Ingredients.—Remains of cold roast beef, ¼ as much mashed potato, 1 cup of gravy, breadcrumbs, seasoning of pepper, salt, mustard, and ketchup.

Method.—Mince the meat very fine, mix with it the potato, and season well; add the cup of gravy, work altogether and make very hot in a saucepan Pile upon a dish, cover with fine breadcrumbs, and brown quickly in the oven. It is much improved by putting bits of butter over the top as it begins to brown. Serve in the dish it is baked in.

Breakfast Dish of Beef.

Ingredients.—Cold roast beef, 3 tablespoonfuls of melted butter, 1 tablespoonful of walnut ketchup, 1 teaspoonful of vinegar, a little salt and pepper, a dessertspoonful of currant jelly, and a little warm water.

Method.—Cut thin slices of cold roast beef, and lay them in a tin saucepan set in a pot of boiling water, and cover them with a gravy made of the above ingredients. Cover tightly, and steam for half-an-hour, keeping the water in the outer vessel on a hard boil. If the meat is underdone, this is particularly nice.

Beef Croquettes.

Ingredients.—Minced cold beef, boiled or roast, a quarter as much mashed potato, gravy enough to moisten them, in which an onion has been boiled and strained out, season with ketchup, pepper, salt, and a pinch of marjoram, fine breadcrumbs, and 1 egg.

Method.—Mash the potatoes, while hot, very smooth, or if cold potatoes be used, see they are free from lumps; mix in the meat, gravy, and seasoning, bind all together with the beaten egg, and form into the desired shapes; roll them in fine breadcrumbs, and fry quickly to a light brown. Drain on soft paper before the fire till free from fat, and serve hot.

Stewed Breast of Lamb.

Ingredients.—One breast of lamb, pepper and salt to taste, sufficient stock to cover it, thickening of butter and flour.

Method.—Skin the lamb and cut it into pieces, and season them with pepper and salt; lay these in a stewpan with sufficient stock or gravy to cover them, and stew gently for an hour and a-half. Just before serving, thicken the gravy with a little butter and flour, give one boil, and pour it over the meat. Have ready a pint and a-half of green peas and lay them over and around the meat. A few stewed mushrooms will be found an improvement if they can be obtained, but they are not necessary for this dish.

Minced Lamb, with Poached Eggs.

Ingredients.—Remains of cold roast lamb, 1 good cup of gravy, pepper, salt, seasoning of mint, poached eggs, buttered toast.

Method.—Trim the meat and mince it finely, well season with pepper, salt, and a little mint. Put the gravy into a saucepan (make it from the bones if you have no other), and let it get hot; then stir in the mince, and let all become very hot, but do not let it boil, thicken with a little browned flour, and pile on a flat dish. Have ready a few slices of buttered toast, cut into neat squares, lay a poached egg on each, place these around or upon the mince, and serve.

Bondinettes of Veal, Rabbit, Chicken, &c.

Ingredients.—Cold meat, potatoes, crumbs, seasoning, and gravy.

Method.—To every pound of finely minced meat, add a ¼ of a pound of mashed potatoes or very fine breadcrumbs, and a little minced parsley or sweet herbs; season with pepper and salt and moisten with a little gravy, which can be made from the bones. Press the mixture into well-buttered cups, and bake in a moderate oven for twenty minutes. Turn on to a hot dish, pour a little browned gravy round, and stick a sprig of parsley into each bondinette.

Pulled Turkey.

Ingredients.—Remains of cold roast or boiled turkey, milk to cover it, thickened with a little flour, a few slices of bacon, rolled and toasted.

Method.—Take the remains of a roast or boiled turkey, and *pull* the white part of the meat from the bones with a fork, so that it is in small strips. Put this into a saucepan, and cover with milk, thickened with a little flour. (A sprig of mace steeped in the milk, and removed before it is thickened, will be found an improvement.) In the meantime joint and grill the leg, lay this on a hot dish, pour the *pulled* turkey round, garnish with a few small rolls of bacon, and serve.

Turkey Scallop.

Ingredients.—Remains of cold roast or boiled turkey, breadcrumbs, butter.

Method.—Crack the carcase, and put it with skin, fat, and gristle, into a saucepan, cover with cold water and set on to stew slowly into gravy. Chop the meat very fine; strew the bottom of a greased pie-dish with crumbs, next a thick stratum of minced turkey, stuffing and bits of butter, pepper and salt. Proceed in this order until the dish is full, reserve enough fine crumbs for a crust, and set this aside till the gravy is ready. When the gravy has drawn all the goodness from the bones, strain it and return it to the saucepan, boil up, thickened with a little browned flour wet with milk, pour it over the scallop, saving a little to wet the top. Now comes a layer of *fine* breadcrumbs. Wet these with gravy into a smooth paste, season with pepper and salt and spread evenly over the scallop. Cover with a dish and bake for half-an-hour, remove the cover, brown, and serve at once.

Rabbit Pie.

Ingredients.—1 rabbit, a few slices of salt pork, 1 hard-boiled egg, a little mace, a few drops of lemon-juice, pepper and butter.

Method.—Cut the rabbit into eight pieces, soak in salted water half-an-hour, and stew until half-done in enough water to cover it. Lay some slices of the pork in the bottom of a pie-dish, and upon these a layer of the rabbit. Upon this lay slices of boiled egg, peppered and buttered. Sprinkle a little powdered mace, and squeeze a few drops of lemon-juice upon each piece of meat. Proceed in this order until the dish is full, the top layer being bacon. Pour in the water in which the rabbit was stewed, and adding a little flour, cover with puff paste, cut a slit in the middle, and bake one hour, laying paper over the top should it brown too fast.

Jugged Rabbits.

Ingredients.—2 rabbits, a few thin slices of salt pork, minced onion and parsley, 1 teacup of gravy, a dessert-spoonful of currant jelly, a little browned flour.

Method.—Skin, clean with care, and joint the rabbits. Lay some thin slices of salt pork in the bottom of a stoneware jar, lay upon them some pieces of rabbit, and strew with a little minced onion and parsley; add more pork, more rabbit, &c., till all is used up. Pour over this a cupful of gravy, cover the jar closely, and stand it in the oven. Cook steadily for two hours, or longer if the meat is not tender. When it is done, arrange the meat on a hot dish; strain the gravy into a basin, and stand it in a basin of cold water for a minute, to throw up the fat; remove this, add a dessert-spoonful of currant jelly, a little browned flour wet with water, boil up and pour over the rabbits. Serve quite hot.

Note.—To make this dish especially good, lay the rabbit when it is cut up in milk and water for several hours, or all night; and serve a few small forcemeat balls in the gravy. It is then an excellent and inexpensive substitute for jugged hare.

To Cook an Old Fowl.

Skin the fowl and cut it up; place it in a stewpan with just enough water to cover it, and let it stew gently till the bones can be easily taken from the meat. The time required for this will depend a good deal on the age of the fowl, but four or five hours will generally do. When done, remove the bones, mince the meat, and flavour it to taste with pepper, salt, cayenne, nutmeg, and grated lemon peel. Return it to the stewpan with the broth, mix all well together, and boil for about five minutes. Pour it into a plain mould till quite cold, then turn it out and garnish with parsley. This will be found an excellent dish for supper or breakfast.

Another Way.—Prepare the fowl as above, put it into a deep dish with a few thin slices of salt pork and just enough water to cover it, and place another dish upon the top, to keep the steam in. Stand this in a moderately hot oven in the evening, and let it remain all night. Next morning make it into a pie in the following manner:—Line a dish with pastry, and arrange the fowl, pork, and slices of a hard-boiled egg, peppered, in alternate layers, till the dish is full; cover with a crust, and bake for about an hour.

The above recipes will be found extremely useful

MEAT AND POULTRY.

for cooking fowls which are too old for roasting or boiling in the usual manner.

Potted Chicken.

Ingredients.—¼ lb. cold roast chicken, 2 oz. ham, 2 oz. fresh butter, ½ teaspoonful of pounded mace, ¼ of a small nutmeg, salt and cayenne to taste.

Method.—Cut the ham and chicken into small pieces, taking out any pieces of skin, pound it with the butter, gradually add the spices, and keep pounding until reduced to a smooth paste. Put into pots and cover with clarified butter, and, if to be kept for some time, tie down with paper.

Chicken Pâtés.

Ingredients.—Remains of cold roast fowls, stuffing of the same, 3 tablespoonfuls of milk, 1 oz. of butter rolled in flour, pepper and salt; pastry.

Method.—Line some pâté tins with good pastry, and bake to a very light brown. Mince the cold chicken, put the bones and stuffing into a saucepan with ½ pint of water, and stew this down to half the quantity, remove the bones, add the milk, and butter and season; stir in the chicken, make it very hot, but do not let it boil. Slip the pastry from the tins, and arrange them on a hot dish; fill with the mixture, and set in the oven till they are sent to table.

Note.—For pâté cases made without the tins, see " Fish Pâtés."

Minced Chicken and Eggs.

Ingredients.—Remains of cold roast or boiled fowl, stuffing of the same, 1 onion cut fine, 1 teacup of milk, 1 tablespoonful of flour or cornflour, parsley, salt and pepper, breadcrumbs, eggs to cover the top of the dish.

Method.—Cut the meat of the fowls into neat squares. Put the bones, fat, and skin into a saucepan, with enough water to cover them, and stew gently for an hour or more. Strain, let it stand a little while for the fat to rise, skim, and return to the saucepan. When nearly boiling, add the milk (thickened with flour) and the seasoning. As soon as it thickens put in the chicken; let it get hot, but do not allow it to boil again. Butter a deep pie-dish, cover the bottom of it with the stuffing (crumbled up), wet with a little gravy, and pour in the mince; then strew fine breadcrumbs over, and lay the eggs (broken into separate cups) carefully over the surface. Strew *very fine* crumbs over these, put some butter, pepper, and salt on each egg, and bake in a quick oven till the top begins to bubble and smoke. The whites of the eggs should be well set, and the yolks soft.

Note.—Cold fowl served in this manner makes an elegant and savoury dish for dinner or supper. A mince of veal may be made in the same way, in which case a little ham will be found an improvement.

Curries.

Ingredients.—1½ lbs. of steak, or veal cutlets, 2 ozs. butter, or good beef-dripping, 2 onions, 1 apple, 1 tablespoonful of curry-powder, 1 tablespoonful of flour, salt to taste, ½ pint of water or gravy, and the juice of a lemon.

Method.—Slice the onions and apple, and fry them in the butter to a light brown. Cut the meat into neat squares, mix the curry-powder, flour, and salt together on a plate, rub each piece of meat into it, and fry quickly. Turn all into a saucepan with the water or gravy, which should be hot, and *simmer* gently for 1½ hour; add the lemon-juice, and serve in a meat dish, with a border of boiled rice piled round.

Note.—Cold beef or mutton may be curried in the same manner, but gravy, not water, should then be used. For curried fowl, substitute boiling milk for the gravy.

To Boil Rice for Curries.

Wash ½ a pound of rice, and throw it into a saucepan of boiling water, which should be salted, and boil for twenty minutes, stirring frequently, that it may not burn. When done, strain it through a sieve, and pour over it some more boiling water to rinse it; place it on the sieve before the fire, and cover with a cloth, and let it stand for a quarter-of-an-hour to dry, taking care to keep it hot. It should then be quite white, and every grain separate, not clinging together as in a pudding. Patna rice is the best for curries.

Camp Pie.

Ingredients.—Cold beef or mutton, pepper and salt, seasoning of ketchup or Worcester sauce, and ½ an onion if liked.

Method.—Mince the meat very fine, add pepper, salt, and the onion finely chopped. Make gravy of the bones and flavour it with ketchup or Worcester sauce; mix this with the minced meat, put it into a pie-dish, cover with a tolerably thick layer of mashed potatoes, well seasoned with pepper and salt, and bake for an hour.

Devilled Meat.

Ingredients.—Cold meat, fowl or kidneys, 1 teaspoonful of made mustard, 2 teaspoonfuls of Worcester sauce, 2 teaspoonfuls of ketchup, 1 teaspoonful of Chili vinegar, ¼ teaspoonful of cayenne, 1 teaspoonful of salad oil, 1 small teaspoonful of lemon-juice, a little bit of butter and a wineglass of claret.

Method.—Cut the meat into slices and lay it on a dish; make a sauce of the above ingredients, pour this over it and set it in a hot oven for fifteen minutes, stirring frequently. Serve with mashed potatoes.

Note.—This will be appreciated only by those who can relish a *very hot* dish.

Fried Kidneys.

Ingredients.—3 large kidneys, 3 tablespoonfuls of butter, ½ teacup good brown gravy, 1 teaspoonful of chopped parsley, ⅓ teaspoonful of minced onion, pepper and salt.

Method.—Skin the kidneys, and cut crosswise into round slices a quarter of an inch thick, then roll them in flour. Have ready in a frying-pan the butter, well seasoned with pepper, salt, parsley, and onion. When it begins to simmer over the fire, lay in carefully and evenly the slices of kidney. Fry gently for two minutes, turn, and let them fry as long on the other side, or until they are of a light brown. If cooked too much or too fast they become tough and tasteless. Remove instantly from the frying-pan with an egg-slice, and arrange on a hot dish. Add to the gravy in the pan a few tablespoonfuls of broth, thickened with browned flour, boil up once, pour over the kidneys, and serve.

Toasted Kidneys.

Ingredients.—3 kidneys, skinned and split lengthwise, each into 3 pieces, ¼ lb. fat pork, cut into slices, pepper and salt, slices or rounds of toasted bread from which the crust has been pared.

Method.—Lay the kidneys upon a *very hot* plate —a tin one is best—in front of, and on a level with, a clear brisk fire. Toast the pork on a fork slice by slice, holding it so that the gravy will drip upon the kidneys beneath. When the pork is done, lay it upon another hot plate, and set in the place just occupied by the kidneys. Toast the kidneys in their turn, so that all the gravy falls upon the pork, turn them frequently, and take care not to lose a drop of the gravy. When the gravy ceases to flow the kidneys are done. Serve upon the toast in a hot dish; cut the pork into strips and lay it along the sides, pour over the gravy, and serve. Pepper and salt just before sending to table.

Broiled Kidneys.

Ingredients.—2 kidneys, 2 tablespoonfuls of melted butter, pepper and salt, and a little chopped parsley.

Method.—Skin the kidneys carefully, but do not slice or split them. Lay for ten minutes in *warm* (not hot) melted butter, rolling them over and over, that every part may be well basted. Broil on a gridiron over a clear fire, turning them every minute. They should be done in about twelve minutes, unless very large. Sprinkle with salt and pepper, and lay on a hot dish with a bit of butter upon each. Cover and send up immediately.

Stewed Kidneys.

Ingredients.—3 kidneys, 3 tablespoonfuls melted butter, juice of half lemon, and a pinch of grated lemon-peel. A very little mace, and pepper and salt to taste, 1 teaspoonful chopped onion, 1 cup good brown gravy.

Method.—Cut each kidney lengthwise into three

pieces; wash these well and wipe dry. Warm the butter in a saucepan; put in the kidneys before this is really hot, with the seasoning and gravy. Simmer all together, closely covered, about ten minutes. Add the lemon-juice; take up the kidneys and lay upon a hot dish, with fried or toasted bread underneath. Thicken the gravy with browned flour, boil up once, pour over all, and serve.

Kidneys à la Brochette.

Ingredients.—4 kidneys (those of medium size are preferable to large), 2 great spoonfuls of butter, 1 great spoonful chopped parsley, onion, and very fine bread crumbs, juice of half a lemon, pepper and salt to taste.

Method.—Split the kidneys lengthwise, but not quite through, leaving enough meat and skin at one side to act as a sort of hinge. Rub them well inside with melted-butter, and lay them open, as you would small birds, the back downwards, upon a buttered gridiron over a bright fire. They should be done in about eight minutes. Turn often while broiling. Have ready the stuffing of crumbs, parsley, onion, and butter, well seasoned. Heat in a saucepan, stirring until smoking hot. Add the lemon-juice, dish the kidneys, put some of this mixture inside of each, close the two sides upon it, butter and pepper them, and serve. A few bits of fat salt pork, minced very fine, gives a good flavour to the stuffing. The pork should have been previously cooked.

Mutton Cutlets.—No. 1:

Ingredients.—Cutlets from the neck of mutton, thin batter of flour and water, slightly salted, fine brown toast raspings, lard or dripping.

Method.—Trim the cutlets and beat them flat with the broad side of a hatchet. Make a little thin batter (on a soup plate if for only a few cutlets) with the flour and water; dip the cutlets into this, then cover them with good brown raspings, and fry quickly in lard or clarified dripping. Drain free from fat on a soft paper before the fire, and serve very hot.

Note.—This recipe saves an egg.

Mutton Cutlets.—No. 2.

Ingredients.—Cutlets, egg, breadcrumbs, lard or dripping.

Method.—Beat them flat with the broad side of a hatchet. Season with pepper and salt. Dip first in beaten egg, then in breadcrumbs. Fry in lard or dripping. Drain perfectly free from the fat, and arrange them, standing on end, and touching one another, around a mound of mashed potatoes.

Baked Breast of Mutton.

Ingredients.—1 breast of mutton, dripping, a little flour, pepper and salt, dry breadcrumbs.

Method.—Sew the mutton up in a very thin cloth, lay it in a saucepan, nearly cover it with cold water, and stew gently, allowing ten minutes to each pound. Take it out, unwrap and lay it in a baking dish, brush over with butter or warm dripping, dredge with flour, and set in the oven for half-an-hour, basting freely with its own broth. A few minutes before taking it up strew thickly with crumbs, fine and dry, dot bits of butter over it, and brown. Serve garnished with slices of beetroot.

Mutton à la Jardinière.

Ingredients.—5 lbs. of mutton (breast or neck) in one piece, 2 onions, 1 carrot, 2 turnips, 1 pint of tinned tomatoes, a few sprigs of cauliflower, 1 head of celery, pepper and salt, 1 tablespoonful of cornflour, dripping.

Method.—Peel the onion, carrot, and turnip, wash, trim, and divide the celery lengthwise, add the cauliflower, and lay all these in cold water. Next, fry the mutton (whole) in a large frying-pan with some good dripping, till it is lightly browned on both sides, then put it into a deep saucepan with the vegetables (leaving out the tomatoes), cover with cold water and stew, closely covered, for an hour after it begins to simmer; then take out the vegetables and set them aside to cool, add boiling water to the meat if it is not covered, and let it continue to simmer for two hours longer. Pour off the gravy, except about a cupful, cover and leave it where it will keep quite hot. Strain the gravy that has been poured off, and set it in a pan of cold water to throw up the fat, skim it, and pour it into a saucepan with the tomatoes, and let all boil fast, skimming two or three times, till it is reduced to one-half the original quantity or just enough to half cover the meat, season with pepper and salt; stir in a little cornflour (previously mixed with a little cold water), and pour this all into the saucepan with the meat; then let it simmer again. In the meantime cut up the cooled vegetables into neat dice; put a good piece of dripping in a saucepan, and when it is hot stir in the vegetables; shake all together till smoking hot, and leave for a few minutes while the meat is taken up. Lay it in the centre of a large flat dish, pour all the gravy over it, then arrange the vegetables in small mounds around it and serve.

Jellied Tongue.

Ingredients.—1 large boiled tongue, 1½ ozs. gelatine, dissolved in ½ a pint of water, 2 teacups of rich browned veal gravy, 1 bunch of savoury herbs, 1 tablespoonful of sugar, 1 tablespoonful of burnt sugar, for colouring, 1 tablespoonful of ketchup, 1 pint of boiling water, 1 egg, boiled hard.

Method.—Put together the gravy, sugar, ketchup, the burnt sugar, dissolved in a little cold water, and the herbs. Add to this the *gelatine*, then the boiling water, and strain through flannel; let the jelly cool and begin to thicken. Wet a plain mould with cold water, put a very little jelly in the bottom, and arrange the slices of hard-boiled egg in it, pour in a little more jelly, then a layer of tongue; more jelly and tongue, and so on till the mould is filled. Cover and set in a cold place till quite firm. To turn it out, dip the mould in hot water for an instant, invert upon a dish, and garnish with celery or parsley or nasturtium flowers. This makes a very ornamental dish for breakfast or supper. In serving, cut with a thin, sharp knife perpendicularly.

Note.—The remains of cold tongue or fowl may be served in this manner, only using less jelly according to the quantity of meat.

Veal Pâtés.

Ingredients.—Cold roast veal, cold ham, pepper, salt, lemon-peel, a little gravy and milk; pastry.

Method.—Mince some cold roast meat very fine, also some ham, and mix with the veal in the proportion of two-thirds veal and one-third ham; season to taste with pepper, salt, and a little lemon-peel, and wet well with gravy and a little milk. Bake quickly in pâté tins lined with puff paste. If eaten hot, send to table in the tins; if cold, slip them out and pile them on a dish, with sprigs of parsley between.

Jellied Veal.

Ingredients.—2 lbs. of knuckle of veal, shallots, pepper, salt, mace, and thyme to taste.

Method.—Wash the veal and cut it into three pieces. Boil it *slowly*, until the meat will slip easily from the bones—three to four hours; take it out of the liquor, remove all the bones and chop the meat fine, add the seasoning, seeing first that the shallots are also chopped very fine. Put back into the liquor, boil until it is almost dry and can be stirred with difficulty. Turn into a mould, and stand aside till next day. Serve cold, cut in slices and garnished with parsley. The juice of a lemon, stirred in just before it is taken from the fire, is an improvement.

Veal Scallop.

Ingredients.—Cold roast or boiled veal, breadcrumbs, pepper and salt, a little butter, and 1 egg.

Method.—Chop some cold roast or stewed veal very fine, put a layer in the bottom of a buttered pudding-dish, and season with pepper and salt. Next have a layer of finely-powdered bread raspings. Strew some bits of butter upon it, and wet with a little milk; then more veal, seasoned as before, and another round of bread raspings, with butter and milk. When the dish is full, wet well with gravy or broth, diluted with warm water. Spread over all a thick layer of raspings, seasoned with salt, wet into a paste with milk, and bound with a beaten egg or two, if the dish be large. Stick butter-bits thickly over it; invert a tin pan so as to cover all, and keep in the steam, and bake. If small, half-an-hour; three-quarters will suffice for a large dish. Remove the cover ten minutes before it is served, and brown.

Mock Pigeons (Veal).

Ingredients.—2 slices from a fillet of veal, breadcrumbs, a little chopped ham or bacon, pepper, salt, ketchup, a very little thyme and parsley, browned flour, 2 cups of gravy or stock.

Method.—Take the bones from the fillets—which should be about an inch thick—flatten them with a hatchet, and spread each with a forcemeat made of the breadcrumbs, ham, and herbs, and season with pepper and salt. Roll the meat up and bind into oblong rolls with soft string; lay it in a deep dish and pour over it two cups of gravy or stock; turn another dish over them, and bake nearly two hours, basting well with the gravy. When done, lay them on a hot dish, thicken the gravy with browned flour, and season it with pepper, salt, and ketchup. Boil up, pour part over the pigeons and serve the rest in a tureen. The string must be cut and removed before sending to table, but in so doing care must be taken that the shape of the pigeons is not spoiled.

Veal Cutlets (Stewed).

Ingredients.—2 lbs. of veal cutlets, 1 small onion sliced, 4 tablespoonfuls of tomato sauce, salt and pepper, with a bunch of sweet herbs, ½ teacup of gravy, enough butter or clear dripping to fry the cutlets.

Method.—Trim the cutlets and fry them till of a light brown, but *not* crisp; take them out and put them in a covered saucepan. Have ready the gravy in another saucepan, with the tomato sauce stirred into it; fry the sliced onion in the fat from which you have taken the cutlets, and add this with the fat to the gravy. Put in the pepper, salt, and herbs, pour over the cutlets, and simmer, covered, for twenty minutes.

Veal Cake.

Ingredients.—Slices of cooked or uncooked veal, slices of boiled ham, 2 eggs (boiled hard), enough stock or gravy to fill up the mould, and gelatine to set it, small forcemeat balls, pepper and salt.

Method.—Butter a plain round or oval mould, and line the bottom and sides with slices of egg and forcemeat balls, arranged according to taste, then nearly fill it with layers of veal and ham, taking care to season with pepper and salt. If the stock or gravy is not stiff enough to set, add a little gelatine previously soaked in cold water, and melt it over the fire. Fill up the mould with this, and bake for an hour in a moderate oven. Stand it aside till quite cold, turn it out and garnish with parsley and a little of the jelly.

PUDDINGS AND SWEETS.

Puff Paste.

Ingredients.—1 lb. flour, 6 oz. butter, 6 oz. lard, *rather less* than ½ pint of water.

Method.—If the butter is very salt, it should be washed in cold water, then well squeezed to extract all the moisture. See that the flour is quite dry and free from lumps, then mix it into a smooth paste with the water, using a knife for this purpose, and taking care not to make it too wet, or the paste will be tough. Turn it on to a well-floured pastry-board and roll it out till it is about an inch thick, spread it with equal parts of butter and lard, sift over it a very little flour; fold it up, roll out again, and spread more butter and lard as before. Do this three or four times, till all the butter and lard are used, taking care to flour both paste and rolling-pin to prevent them sticking. Brushing the paste as often as rolled out, and the butter that is spread upon it, with the white of an egg, helps it to rise in flakes or leaves, but this is not always done. In **very cold** weather the butter should be mashed on a plate with a knife till it is just soft enough to spread easily; this may be done in a warm place, but care must be taken that it does not oil. To insure light pastry, make it in a cool place, as quickly as possible, and bake in a brisk oven; a cool oven will spoil it, however well made. It is none the worse for being made the day before it is baked, if it is rolled up and left in a cool dry place.

Short Crust for Pies.—No. 1.

Ingredients.—1 lb. flour, 8 oz. butter, yolks of 2 eggs, ¼ pint of water, or rather less.

Method.—See that the flour is quite dry, then rub into it the butter, which should be cool and firm. When it is quite free from lumps, mix it into a smooth paste with the eggs—well beaten—and the water, taking great care that it is not too wet. The dryer it is made the shorter and lighter will the crust be. Roll out on a floured pastry-board, two or three times, folding it each time, and it will be ready for use. Bake in a brisk oven.

Short Crust.—No. 2.

Ingredients.—1 lb. flour, 6 oz. butter, 4 oz. lard, 1 tablespoonful of white pounded sugar, ¾ of pint of water.

Method.—Proceed as in the foregoing recipe.

Apple Meringue Pudding.

Ingredients.—1 pint of stewed apples, 3 eggs—whites and yolks separate—½ teacup white sugar, 1 teaspoonful of butter, ¼ teaspoonful of essence of almond (for the *méringue*).

Method.—Prepare the apples as for a pie, and stew till almost a pulp, sweeten and spice, and while hot stir in the yolks of the eggs gradually. Beat very light, pour into a buttered dish, and bake for ten minutes. Cover, without drawing it from the oven, with a *méringue* made of the beaten whites, 2 tablespoonfuls of white sugar, and the almond flavouring. Spread it over with a tablespoon, evenly and quickly, close the oven again, and brown very slightly. Serve either hot or cold, as preferred.

Note.—In making all *Méringues*, see that the eggs are quite fresh, whip them in a *cool* place, and on a *cold* dish, otherwise they will not rise properly. Use them as soon as they are whipped to a high snowy heap; if left to stand they will become flat, and it is impossible to well froth them a second time. It must also be remembered that the whites will *not* froth to stiffness, if a drop of the yolk is mixed with them.

Baked Apple Pudding.

Ingredients.—6 large apples (grated), 3 tablespoonfuls of butter, ¼ lb. sugar, 2 eggs (whites and yolks beaten separately), juice of one lemon, and half the grated rind; pastry.

Method.—Beat the butter and sugar into a cream, stir in the yolks, the lemon, the grated apple, and lastly the whites of the eggs. Line a dish with pastry, pour in the mixture, and baked till nicely browned. This is best cold.

Note.—Normandy pippins may be used for this pudding if liked.

Apple Charlotte.

Ingredients.—Slices of bread and butter, with the crust trimmed off, 6 apples, the grated rind of a lemon and the juice, sugar to taste.

Method.—Butter a pie-dish, and place a layer of bread-and-butter at the bottom, then a layer of apples, peeled, cored, and cut into slices; sprinkle these over with sugar, a little of the lemon-peel, and a few drops of the juice. Repeat this until the dish is full, then cover it well over with the peel of the apples to prevent it burning, and bake in a quick oven about three-quarters of an hour. When done, remove the peel, turn it out on a dish, sprinkle with white sugar, and serve at once.

Apple Soufflé Pudding.

Ingredients.—6 or 7 fine juicy apples, 1 cup fine breadcrumbs, 4 eggs, 1 cup of sugar, 2 tablespoonfuls butter, nutmeg, and a little grated lemon peel.

Method.—Pare, core, and slice the apples, and stew in a covered double saucepan, without a drop of water, until they are tender. Mash to a smooth pulp, and while hot, stir in the butter and sugar. Let it get quite cold, and whip in, first, the yolks of the eggs, then the whites—beaten *very* stiff—alternately with the bread crumbs. Flavour, beat quickly three minutes, until all the ingredients are reduced to a creamy batter, and bake in a buttered dish, in a moderate oven. It will take about an hour to cook it properly. Keep it covered until ten minutes before you take it out. This will retain the juices and prevent the formation of a crust on the top.

Apple Fritters.

Ingredients.—Apples. *For a batter:* ½ lb. flour, ½ oz. butter, ½ teaspoonful of salt, 2 eggs—whites and yolks beaten separately, milk enough to make it tolerably thin.

Method.—Prepare some apples, as for a pie, or mince them if preferred; add these to the batter, and drop a large tablespoonful at a time into a pan of boiling lard or clarified dripping; fry till of a light brown, turning when required. When done, lay them on a sheet of blotting-paper before the fire to absorb the grease, then dish them, piled high, one above the other, and strewed with sifted sugar. They should be served as hot as possible.

Swiss Apple Pudding.

Ingredients.—Apples, breadcrumbs, moist sugar, butter.

Method.—Prepare the apples as for a pie, and put a layer of them in a buttered dish; cover with breadcrumbs, and a little sugar, and a few small pieces of butter. Repeat this until the dish is full, and bake till well browned. When finished, turn it out of the dish and sprinkle with white sugar.

Agra Pudding.

Ingredients.—4 eggs, 1½ pint of milk, 1 tablespoonful of sugar, vanilla to taste, bread-and-butter, marmalade, and 1 pint of boiled custard.

Method.—Cut thin slices of bread-and-butter, and spread them with the marmalade. Fit them neatly into a buttered pie-dish until it is half full; then pour over them gradually a hot custard, made of the milk heated almost to boiling, then take off the fire, and the beaten eggs and sugar stirred in with the flavouring. Place a small plate on the top to prevent the bread from rising, and let it soak for half-an-hour. Grate a little nutmeg on the top, and bake, and when done turn it out of the dish, and pour over it a pint of *boiled custard*. This pudding is very good, either hot or cold, especially so if French bread can be used.

Note.—A plainer pudding may be made by omitting two of the eggs and the *boiled custard*, but in that case it should be sent to table in the dish in which it is baked. Both are very good.

Arrowroot Charlotte.

Ingredients.—2 tablespoonfuls of flour, 3 tablespoonfuls of arrowroot, 1 quart of milk, flavoured with vanilla, 3 or 4 stale sponge cakes.

Method.—Line a mould with the sponge cakes, cut thin and sprinkled with sherry. Mix the flour and arrowroot with enough cold milk to make it smooth. Put the remainder of the milk into a saucepan and stir in the mixture just before it boils; boil a few minutes, stirring all the time, then pour it boiling into the mould. Stand it aside till quite cold, turn it out of the mould and spread it with jelly or jam.

Arrowroot Creams.

Ingredients.—1 oz. of arrowroot, 3 ozs. powdered sugar, the yolk of 1 egg, 1 quart of milk, a little lemon-peel and cinnamon.

Method.—Mix the arrowroot with a little of the milk to a smooth paste and add to it the egg. Boil the remainder of the milk with the sugar and flavouring, and pour it boiling hot on to the arrowroot, keeping it well stirred till nearly cold, when it may be set aside in custard glasses.

Austrian Pudding.

Ingredients.—1 lb. of flour, a pinch of salt, 1 large teaspoonful of baking powder, ¼ lb. finely-chopped suet, 1 tablespoonful of sugar, 1 breakfastcup of milk, 1 breakfastcup of treacle.

PUDDINGS AND SWEETS.

Method.—Mix the dry ingredients together, then warm the milk, stir it into the treacle, and add it to the pudding. Mix well and boil in a well-buttered basin for three hours.

Bread Fritters.

Ingredients.—1 pint milk, 1 egg, ¼ lb. flour, bread, jam.

Method.—Make a batter with the milk, egg, and flour. Cut some slices of bread rather thin, in squares or three-cornered pieces, spread half of them with jam and cover with the other slices; dip them into the batter, and fry in boiling lard till of a light brown colour. Serve very hot, piled on a dish, and sprinkled with white sugar.

Bread-and-Butter Pudding (Boiled).

Ingredients.—4 eggs well beaten, 1 oz. of lump sugar, ¼ lb. of currants, ¼ of a teaspoonful of salt.

Method.—Butter a basin well, put in a sprinkle of currants all round, then a layer of bread-and-butter, and so on, until the basin or mould be nearly full· then add to the eggs a quart of milk with the sugar. Boil for an hour-and-a-half gently.

Betsy Pudding.

Ingredients.—1 pint of milk, 3 oz. breadcrumbs, 1 egg, 1 tablespoonful of white sugar, jam.

Method.—Spread a good layer of jam in the bottom of a pie-dish. Pour the milk nearly boiling on to the breadcrumbs; when cool stir in the egg, which should be beaten; pour this gently on the preserve; grate a little nutmeg over the top, and bake for half-an-hour.

Bachelor's Pudding.

Ingredients.—1 egg, with its weight in minced apple, flour, sugar, currants, breadcrumbs, suet.

Method.—Mix these with the egg and add a little milk. Boil in a mould from one-and-a-half to two hours.

Carrot Pudding.

Ingredients.—¼ lb. grated carrots, ¼ lb. breadcrumbs, ¼ lb. suet, ¼ lb. flour, ¼ lb. currants or sultanas, 1 large tablespoonful of treacle, ¼ of the rind of a lemon grated.

Method.—Mix well together with a little milk, and boil in a basin, or mould, for an hour-and-a-half.

Christmas Pudding.—No. 1.

Ingredients.—2½ lb. flour, 1½ lb. breadcrumbs, 1½ lb. suet, 1½ lb. raisins, 1 lb. currants, 1 lb. sugar, a little candied peel, 6 eggs, ½ pint of milk.

Method.—Sift the breadcrumbs, chop the suet very fine, stone the raisins, wash and dry the currants, slice the peel. Mix all the dry ingredients well together, then thoroughly beat the eggs, add them to the milk and pour them over the mass. Stir well until all the ingredients are well mixed, butter a mould or basin and fill it, tie down safely and boil for twelve hours.

Christmas Pudding.—No. 2.

Ingredients.—1½ lb. raisins, 1½ lb. currants, 1½ lb. sugar, ¾ lb. flour, ¾ lb. breadcrumbs, 6 oz. candied peel, 1½ lb. suet, 7 or 8 eggs, a few chopped almonds, 1½ wineglasses of brandy, 1½ wineglasses sherry, 1½ wineglasses Noyau, a little salt.

Method.—Proceed as for the foregoing recipe, adding the wine, &c., last. Make into three puddings, and boil in moulds or basins for five hours.

Christmas Pudding.—No. 3 (Impromptu).

Ingredients.—2 cups of best mincemeat made for Christmas pies (if it is too dry for pies, it will make the better pudding), 1½ cups flour, 6 eggs—whites and yolks beaten separately.

Method.—Whip the eggs and stir the yolks into the mincemeat. Beat them in hard for two or three minutes until thoroughly incorporated. Put in the whites and the flour, alternately, beating in each before adding the next. Butter a large mould very well, put in the mixture, leaving room for the swelling of the pudding, and boil five hours steadily. If the boiling should intermit one minute, there will be a heavy streak in the pudding. Six hours' boiling will do no harm. Turn out upon a hot dish and eat with rich sauce if liked.

Citron Pudding.

Ingredients.—4 oz. butter, 3 oz. powdered loaf sugar, 1 egg, candied peel, pastry.

Method.—Soften the butter to a thin cream, beat the egg, add the sugar, then the butter; mix all well together. Line a *shallow* pie-dish with nice pastry, put in the bottom a rather thick layer of citron peel sliced, or citron and lemon mixed, then pour the mixture over it, and bake till the crust is sufficiently done. To be served cold.

Cream Raspberry Pie.

Ingredients.—Puff paste, 1 quart of raspberries, sugar to taste, a good teacupful of milk, a pinch of soda, ½ a teaspoonful of cornflour, 1 tablespoonful of white pounded sugar, whites of 2 eggs.

Method.—Line a pie-dish with puff paste, and fill with raspberries, sweetened to taste. Cover with pastry, but do not press this down at the edges; also rub the edge of the lower crust, to prevent adhesion, and bake in a brisk oven. While it is cooking, heat a small teacupful of milk, with a pinch of soda in it, and stir into it the cornflour, which should be previously wetted with a little cold milk, add the white sugar, and cook for three minutes. Pour the mixture into a small basin, and beat in the frothed whites of 2 eggs; whip to a cream, and let it get cold. When the pie is taken from the oven, lift the top crust, and pour in the cream you have made; replace the crust, and set aside to cool. Sprinkle a little sugar over the top before serving.

Cornflour Hasty Pudding.

Ingredients.—1 quart of milk, 3 tablespoonfuls of cornflour, 1 teaspoonful of salt, 1 tablespoonful of butter.

Method.—Mix the cornflour with a little cold milk to a smooth paste. Put the salt into the rest of the milk, bring it to the boiling point, then pour it over the cornflour, stirring so that it is well mixed. Return it to the saucepan, and boil steadily, stirring frequently, for fifteen minutes; then add the butter. Let the pudding stand in a pan of hot water, uncovered, after you have ceased to stir, till it is served, and send it to table in a deep dish, with cream and sugar, or jam.

Cherry Bread Pudding.

Ingredients.—1 quart of milk with a pinch of soda stirred in, slices of bread and butter, 4 eggs, 1 teacup of sugar, 1 teacup of stoned cherries.

Method.—Trim the slices of bread and butter neatly, put a layer in the bottom of a pie-dish, and pour upon it a little raw custard, made of the beaten eggs, sugar, and milk; strew over this a layer of cherries, then more bread and butter and custard, and proceed in this order till the dish is full, taking care that the top layer is bread, particularly well buttered. Cover with a dish, and let soak for an hour; then set it, still covered, in a pan of hot water, and bake for one hour; then uncover, and brown delicately. Serve hot.

Note.—For a plainer pudding use only 2 eggs.

Cornflour Méringue.

Ingredients.—1 quart of milk, 4 good teaspoonfuls of cornflour, 4 eggs, 2 tablespoonfuls of pounded white sugar, 1 tablespoonful of jelly or jam, flavouring of vanilla or lemon.

Method.—Heat the milk to boiling, and pour it on the cornflour, which should be previously mixed with a little cold milk; boil fifteen minutes, stirring all the time. Remove from the fire, and while still hot add gradually the yolks of the eggs, beaten up with the sugar and flavoured with vanilla or lemon. Pour this into a buttered pudding-dish and bake for about fifteen minutes, or until the custard begins to set. Draw it from the oven and heap lightly and quickly upon it a *méringue* made of the whites of the eggs, whipped to a stiff froth with the jelly or jam, which must be added gradually. Return it to the oven to brown slightly, and serve either hot or cold. Use currant jelly for the *méringue* if the custard is flavoured with vanilla, and strawberry or other sweet jam if lemon is used.

Curate Puddings.

Ingredients.—3 eggs, with their weight in flour, pounded sugar, and butter, flavouring of lemon, almond, or vanilla.

Method.—Warm the butter and beat to a cream gradually dredge in the flour and pounded sugar, and keep stirring and beating the mixture without ceasing until it is perfectly smooth. Then add the eggs, which should be *well whisked*, and either of the above flavourings that may be preferred; butter some small cups or tins, rather more than half fill them, and bake in a brisk oven for about half-an-hour. Turn them out on a dish, and pour custard or wine-sauce round them.

Note.—The paste for these puddings requires a great deal of mixing, and the more it is beaten the better will the puddings be.

Claret Jelly.

Ingredients.—1 oz. gelatine, soaked in cold water, ½ pint of water, 1 pint of claret, ½ lb. loaf sugar, 1 wineglass of brandy, 1 lemon.

Method.—Put soaked gelatine, sugar, and lemon together; pour on the boiling water; stir until melted. Add the wine, and strain, without squeezing, through double flannel. Put in a wet mould, and set in ice. Turn out upon a cold glass dish, and serve cake with it.

Cocoanut Pudding.

Ingredients.—3 oz. butter, ¼ lb. grated cocoanut, 1½ cups of stale sponge cakes, crumbed fine, 3 oz. sugar, 1 large cup of milk, 6 eggs, ½ teaspoonful of vanilla or rosewater.

Method.—Cream the butter and sugar, and add the beaten yolks; when these are well mixed put in the cocoanut; stir well before adding the milk, cake crumbs, and flavouring; lastly, add the *whites of* 3 eggs. Pour the mixture into a pie-dish—which should not be quite full—and bake for half-an-hour. At the end of this time whip the other whites to a very stiff froth, with 3 tablespoonfuls of white sugar, and flavour with vanilla. Pile this in large spoonfuls on the pudding, and close the oven till it is slightly brown. For all *meringues* the oven should be only moderately hot, or they will burn. These quantities are sufficient for a large pudding.

Currant Fritters.

Ingredients.—4 tablespoonfuls of flour, one teacup of currants, ½ pint of milk, 3 eggs—the whites beaten separately.

Method.—Mix all well together, and fry quickly in boiling fat. Drain them before the fire on soft paper, pile them high on a dish, and sprinkle with white sugar.

Delhi Pudding.

Ingredients.—3 tablespoonfuls of arrowroot, 1½ oz. Sweet almonds, pounded, 1 oz. of butter, 1½ pints of milk, 2 tablespoonfuls of sugar.

Method.—Mix the almonds, arrowroot, butter, and sugar in ½ a pint of cold milk; have ready on the fire a pint of milk, when boiling pour it on the above mixture; stir till thick, and stand it aside in a mould till quite cold.

Egg Jelly.

Ingredients.—1 oz. of gelatine, 1 pint of cold water, 1 lemon, ¼ lb. of loaf sugar, yolks of 5 eggs.

Method.—Dissolve the gelatine in the water and stand it aside for an hour; then put it in a stewpan, with the lemon-peel and sugar and let it come to the simmering point. Have ready in a basin the yolks of five eggs, well beaten, and add to them the contents of the stewpan, adding also the juice of the lemon while pouring. Strain through muslin into a mould.

French Pancakes.

Ingredients.—2 eggs, 2 oz. of butter, 2 oz. of sifted sugar, 2 oz. of flour, ½ a pint of new milk.

Method.—Beat the eggs thoroughly, and put them into a basin with the butter, which should be beaten to a cream; stir in the sugar and flour, and when these ingredients are well mixed, add the milk, which should be slightly warm; keep stirring and beating the mixture for a few minutes; put it on buttered plates, and bake it in a quick oven for twenty minutes. Serve with a cut lemon and sifted sugar, or pile the pancakes high on a dish with a layer of preserve or marmalade between each.

Fig Pudding.—No. 1.

Ingredients.—½ lb. of figs, ¼ lb. breadcrumbs, 6 oz. brown sugar, 2 eggs, ¼ lb. suet, 2 oz. flour, nutmeg to taste, a little milk.

Method.—Chop the suet very fine, also the figs, add the flour, breadcrumbs, sugar, nutmeg, and, lastly, the eggs (which should be well beaten), and sufficient milk to mix well. Boil for four hours in a buttered mould or basin. Serve with or without wine-sauce, as preferred.

Note.—Half this quantity *steamed* for three hours makes a delicious pudding.

Fig Pudding.—No. 2.

Ingredients.—½ lb. suet, ½ lb. flour, ½ lb. figs, ¼ lb. sugar, 1 egg, a little milk or water.

Method.—Mix as above, and boil well for three hours.

Fig Custard Pudding.

Ingredients.—½ lb. of good figs, 1 pint of milk, yolks of two eggs, white of one, if *large* ½ oz. of gelatine, soaked in cold water, ½ a cup of sweet fruit jelly, slightly warmed, two tablespoonfuls of white sifted sugar, flavour to taste with vanilla.

Method.—Soak the figs in warm water till quite soft; split them, dip each piece in the jelly, and line a *buttered* mould with them. Heat the milk and stir into it the well-beaten *yolks* and sugar; return it to the saucepan and stir till it thickens. Melt the soaked gelatine by adding a tablespoonful of boiling water, and setting it in a vessel of hot water; when it is quite melted add it to the milk, and when well mixed, set by to cool. As soon as it begins to congeal, whisk it thoroughly with an egg-beater, and add to it gradually the white of an egg, previously whipped to a stiff froth. Beat it rapidly and thoroughly till quite spongy, and fill up the fig-lined mould. Set in a cold place till quite firm, five or six hours at least. Dip the mould in hot water to loosen the pudding, when you are ready for it, and serve on a glass dish. The above quantities will fill a quart mould. It can be made the day before it is required, if convenient to do so.

Floating Island.

Ingredients.—1 quart of milk, 4 eggs (whites and yolks separate), 4 tablespoonfuls of sugar, flavouring of bitter almond or vanilla, ½ a teacup of currant jelly.

Method.—Heat the milk to scalding, but do not let it boil; beat the yolks of the eggs, stir into them the sugar, and pour upon them gradually, and mixing well, a cupful of the hot milk; return it to the saucepan and boil till it begins to thicken, stirring all the time. When cool, flavour and pour into a glass dish, and just before serving heap upon it a *méringue* made of the whites of the eggs, whipped to a stiff froth, with the jelly beaten in, a teaspoonful at a time.

General Satisfaction.

Ingredients.—4 sponge cakes, ½ pint of milk, 3 eggs, a wineglass of sherry, sugar to taste for custard, jam, puff paste, 3 tablespoonfuls of pounded white sugar for the *méringue*.

Method.—Line a pie-dish with puff paste, and spread over the bottom a thick layer of jam (*not a very sweet kind*), lay upon this the sponge cakes, which should be previously soaked in the sherry; pour over them a custard made of the milk and yolks of the eggs slightly sweetened, and bake for one hour. Make a *méringue* of the whites of the eggs and fine pounded sugar, heap this roughly and lightly, upon the pudding, and close the oven door for five or ten minutes to set it. It should be tinged all over with a delicate brown. Serve quite cold.

Note.—Milk may be substituted for the sherry, if desired, and if a *white méringue* is liked, allow the pudding to get quite cold, make the *méringue* only just before it is sent to table, and do not bake it.

German Puffs.

Ingredients.—2 oz. of butter, 3 tablespoonfuls of sugar, 3 eggs—whites and yolks separate—3 teacups of milk, 3 teacups of flour, 1 saltspoonful of salt, and a few drops of vanilla.

Method.—Beat the butter to a cream, add the sugar and well-beaten yolks, then the milk, which should be salted; dredge in the flour by degrees, and when these are well mixed, add the flavouring and whites of the eggs, previously beaten to *stiff froth*. Bake in well-buttered teacups about fifteen or twenty minutes, till of a light brown. As these puffs rise very much, the cups must not be filled. Serve as soon as done, with sweet sauce.

Gingerbread Pudding.

Ingredients.—½ lb. of treacle, ½ lb. of flour, 6 oz. or ¼ lb. of suet, 1 teaspoonful ginger, ½ pint of milk, 1 egg, ¼ teaspoonful carbonate of soda, candied peel to taste.

Method.—Mix the dry ingredients, then add the egg, and the milk in which the soda has been dissolved, and boil in a mould for two hours and a half.

Gooseberry Pudding (Baked).

Ingredients.—1 pint of gooseberries, 1 teacup of milk, ½ teacup of sugar, 1 tablespoonful of butter (melted), toasted bread.

Method.—Stew the gooseberries gently in a little water for about ten minutes. Cut some slices of bread, trim off the crust, and toast it to a light brown. Dip each slice, while hot, into the milk, and spread it with the melted butter. Cover the bottom of the dish with them; next put a layer of gooseberries, sprinkled well with sugar, and so on, till the dish is full. Cover closely, and steam in a moderate oven for twenty or twenty-five minutes; then remove the cover, and let it brown before serving. Serve with good pudding sauce, if liked.

Gooseberry Fool.

Ingredients.—1 pint gooseberry pulp, 1 pint milk, sugar to taste.

Method.—Cut the tops and tails off the gooseberries, and put them into a jar, with 2 tablespoonfuls of water and a little moist sugar; set this in a saucepan of boiling water, and let it boil till the fruit is soft enough to mash. When done enough, beat it to a pulp, and work this pulp through a colander; stir to every pint the above proportion of milk, and plenty of sugar. In mixing, add the milk very gradually to the gooseberries, and serve in a glass dish.

Gooseberry Fool (Rich).

Ingredients.—1 quart gooseberries (*ripe*), 1 tablespoonful of butter, 1 teacup of sugar, 4 eggs, 3 tablespoonfuls of white sugar,

Method.—Stew the gooseberries in just enough water to cover them, and when soft and broken, rub them through a sieve to remove the skins. While still hot, beat in the butter, sugar, and whipped *yolks* of the eggs. Pile in a glass dish, and heap upon the top a *méringue* of the whipped whites and white sugar.

Half-Pay Pudding.

Ingredients.—4 oz. each of suet, flour, currants, raisins, and breadcrumbs; 2 tablespoonfuls of treacle, and ½ pint of milk.

Method.—Mix all well together, and boil in a buttered mould for four hours. May be served with wine or brandy sauce.

Kentish Pudding Pies.

Ingredients.—3 oz. of ground rice, 1½ pints of milk, 2 oz. butter, 4 oz. sugar, 4 eggs, a *little* salt lemon peel or nutmeg.

Method.—Infuse 2 bay leaves, or the rind of ½ a lemon, in the milk, and when it is well flavoured strain it, and add the rice and salt; boil these for quarter-of-an-hour, stirring all the time. Then take them off the fire, stir in the butter, sugar, and eggs, and let the latter be well beaten before they are added to the other ingredients. When nearly cold, line some patty tins with puff paste, fill with the custard, strew a few currants over the top, and bake about twenty minutes in a moderate oven.

Lemon Pie.

Ingredients.—1 apple, chopped fine, 1 egg, 1 lemon—chop the inside very fine and grate the rind —1 teacup of sugar, butter about the size of a walnut.

Method.—Mix the ingredients well together, line a tart-tin with puff paste, fill the centre part with the mixture, and bake a very light brown.

Lemon Creams.

Ingredients.—½ pint of water, the juice of 2 lemons and peel of 1, 3 eggs well beaten, and 6 oz. loaf sugar.

Method.—Put the water, lemon peel, and sugar in a saucepan over the fire, and stir till the sugar is dissolved. Strain through a coarse muslin, and stand aside till cold; then add the lemon juice and eggs, return the mixture to the saucepan, and stir until it thickens; continue stirring until cool, and pour into custard glasses.

Lemon Pudding.

Ingredients.—½ lb. fine breadcrumbs, ¼ lb. finely-chopped suet, ¼ lb. of sifted white sugar, rind of 2 lemons (grated), juice of 1 (strained), 2 eggs.

Method.—Mix together all the dry ingredients, then add the lemon juice, and, lastly, the well-beaten eggs. Boil in a buttered basin for three-quarters-of-an-hour.

Lemon Méringue Pudding.

Ingredients.—1 pint of milk, 1 teacup of breadcrumbs, 2 eggs, 1 oz. butter, ½ a cup of white sugar, 1 *small* lemon, juice and ½ the rind (grated).

Method.—Warm the milk and pour it on the breadcrumbs, add the beaten yolks, with the butter and sugar rubbed to a cream, also the lemon. Bake it in a buttered dish till firm and slightly brown— about half-an-hour. Draw to the door of the oven, and cover lightly with a *méringue* of the whites, whipped to a stiff froth, with 3 tablespoonfuls of powdered sugar and a little lemon juice; brown very slightly, and serve hot or cold, as preferred. Orange pudding may be made in the same way.

Lemon Trifle.

Ingredients.—1 large sponge cake (sliced), 1 quart of milk, 3 eggs (whites and yolks separate), 5 large tablespoonfuls of pounded white sugar, 1 lemon (all the juice), and ¼ of the rind very finely grated, essence of lemon to flavour the *méringue*.

Method.—Slice the cake and arrange it in a deep glass dish, then pour upon it a teacupful of hot milk to soak it. Well beat the yolks of the eggs, and stir with them 4 tablespoonfuls of sugar; heat the rest of the milk and pour it upon the eggs by degrees, stirring all the time; return it to the saucepan and continue stirring till it thickens, let it cool a little, add the strained juice of the lemon and pour over the sponge cake. When perfectly cold, heap upon it a *méringue* made of the whites of the eggs whipped to a stiff froth, sweetened with the other tablespoonful of sugar, and flavoured with essence of lemon and rind.

Note.—The *méringue* should be made just before serving.

Marmalade Pudding (Boiled).

Ingredients.—2 eggs, ¼ lb. breadcrumbs, ¼ lb. suet, ¼ lb. sugar, ¼ lb. marmalade, a little milk.

Method.—Put the breadcrumbs into a basin, and add to them the suet (finely chopped), the marmalade, and sugar; stir these ingredients well together, then add the eggs, which should be previously well beaten; add sufficient milk to well mix the pudding, and boil for two hours in a buttered basin or mould.

Marmalade Pudding (Baked).

Ingredients.—3 oz. butter, 3 oz. white pounded sugar, 3 tablespoonfuls of orange marmalade, 4 eggs, 1 tablespoonful of flour, pastry, a few almonds.

Method.—Beat the butter to a cream, add the sugar, flour, and marmalade, and, lastly, the eggs (well beaten). Beat all well together for ten minutes, line a dish with pastry, pour in the mixture, and bake in a moderate oven for an hour. Stick the pudding with almonds, and serve with custard sauce.

Marmalade Custard Pudding.

Ingredients.—1 teacup of fine breadcrumbs, 1½ cups of milk, 1 tablespoonful of sugar, 2 eggs, 2 teaspoonfuls of butter, 1 teacup of marmalade.

Method.—Beat the butter and sugar together, add the yolks (well beaten), the milk, and breadcrumbs, and, lastly, the whites of the eggs, beaten to a froth. Put a layer of this in a well-buttered dish, spread with marmalade, then another layer of the mixture, and so on, till the dish is full; taking care to have the custard mixture at the top. Bake in a moderate oven about three-quarters-of-an-hour.

Mysterious Pudding.

Ingredients.—2 eggs, and their weight in flour, butter, and castor sugar, a tablespoonful of marmalade, a teaspoonful of baking powder.

Method.—Beat the butter to a cream, and add to it the sugar, then the flour—with which the baking powder should be mixed—and marmalade. Beat the eggs well, yolks and whites separately, adding the whites *lastly*. When the other ingredients are well mixed, pour into a well-buttered basin, and steam for an hour-and-a-half. Turn out, spread a little marmalade over the top, and serve with sweet sauce poured round it.

Newark Pudding.

Ingredients.—1 pint of milk, 2 eggs, 1 tablespoonful of ground rice, ¼ lb. raisins, stoned and cut in two, half a cup of breadcrumbs soaked in ½ a pint of the milk, 1 tablespoonful of melted butter, ¼ teaspoonful of soda, sugar, and vanilla flavouring to taste.

Method.—Beat the yolks light; add the soaked crumbs and milk; stir to a smooth batter, add the rice, wetting first with a little cold milk; add the rest of the milk, seasoning, butter, raisins, and a tablespoonful of sugar; lastly, the whites, well whisked. Bake an hour in a buttered dish, turn out, and serve with sweet sauce.

Orange Fritters.

Ingredients.—3 or 4 oranges. *For the batter:* ½ lb. flour, ½ oz. butter, ¼ teaspoonful of salt, 2 eggs, and enough milk to make it the proper consistency—not *very* thin.

Method.—Peel the oranges, remove as much of the white skin as possible, and divide each into four pieces, without breaking the thin skin, except to remove the pips; dip each piece of orange in the batter. Have ready a pan of *boiling* lard or clarified dripping, drop in the oranges, and fry from eight to ten minutes, to a delicate brown. When done, lay them on a piece of blotting-paper to absorb the fat, taking care, however, to keep them hot; pile high on a dish, strew with white sugar, and serve. These fritters are best when fried in a *saucepan,* as the boiling fat rising closely round them improves the shape.

Orange Pudding (Boiled.)

Ingredients.—2 oranges, juice of both and rind of one, juice of 1 lemon, ¼ lb. stale cake, sponge or Madeira, 2 teacups of milk, 2 eggs, ¼ teacup of white sugar, 1 tablespoonful of cornflour, mixed

PUDDINGS AND SWEETS.

with a little water, 1 tablespoonful of butter, melted.

Method.—Soak the crumbs in the cold milk, whip up lightly, add the eggs and sugar beaten to a cream with the butter; next the cornflour, and when the mould is buttered and the water ready boiling, stir in the juice and peel of the fruit. Do this quickly, tie down, and boil *at once* for an hour. Serve with very sweet sauce, or wine sauce.

Orange Jelly.

Ingredients.—Juice of 7 oranges, rind of 4, juice and rind of a lemon, ½ lb. of loaf sugar, 1 oz. of gelatine, dissolved in ½ pint of water.

Method.—Add the oranges, lemon, and sugar to the dissolved gelatine, boil for ten minutes, strain and set in a mould till cold.

Pearl Barley Pudding.—No. 1.

Ingredients.—¼ lb. pearl barley, 3 pints of water, ½ teaspoonful of salt, 3 tablespoonfuls of sugar, 2 large juicy apples.

Method.—Put the barley into the water and boil gently for two hours, add the salt and sugar, and pour it into a pie-dish. Pare and cut up two large apples, stir these into the pudding, and bake for an hour. Serve with sweet sauce.

Pearl Barley Pudding.—No. 2.

Ingredients.—2 oz. best pearl barley, 1 quart milk, 5 oz. moist sugar.

Method.—Soak the barley in cold water for twelve hours, then drain the water away, put the barley into a pudding-dish, mix the sugar with it, then the milk, sprinkle a little nutmeg on the top, and bake *slowly* from three to three-and-a-half hours; when properly baked it should be of the consistence of very thick cream, and is a most nutritious and agreeable pudding.

The Queen of Puddings.

Ingredients.—2 teacups of breadcrumbs, 1 lemon (the rind grated), 1 pint milk heated, 2 eggs (whites and yolks separate), sugar to taste for pudding; 3 tablespoonfuls of white pounded sugar for the *méringue*, 2 teaspoonfuls of brandy, 4 teaspoonfuls of sherry.

Method.—Soak the breadcrumbs in the milk, add the lemon rind and beaten yolks of the eggs, sweeten to taste, well mix, and pour into a buttered pie-dish, and bake till the custard is set. Spread with jam, and then heap upon it a *méringue* made of the whites of the eggs whipped to a stiff froth, sweetened with the white sugar, flavoured with the lemon juice, brandy, and wine. Set in the oven for five or ten minutes to slightly colour, and serve either hot or cold. In making the *méringue*, mix the liquid flavouring with the sugar before adding it to the eggs. The wine and brandy may be omitted if desired.

The Queen of Puddings, with Strawberry Méringue.

Ingredients.—1 dessertspoonful of butter, 1 tablespoonful of sugar, 2 eggs, 2 teacups of breadcrumbs, 1 pint of milk, lemon flavouring, 2 tablespoonfuls of white sugar for the *méringue*, ½ pint of fresh strawberries.

Method.—Cream the butter, and add to it the sugar and whipped *yolks*, then the crumbs soaked in milk, and lastly the flavouring. Fill a pie-dish two-thirds full, and bake till the custard is set. Draw to the mouth of the oven, and cover with the strawberries rolled in sugar, then with a *méringue* made of the whipped whites and sugar. Close the oven door for a few minutes to colour the *méringue*, and serve cold.

Queen's Toast.

Ingredients.—Bread, sugar, lard for frying.

Method.—Fry slices of baker's bread in boiling lard to a fine light brown. Dip each slice quickly in boiling water to remove the grease, sprinkle with powdered sugar, and pile on a hot dish. Before toasting, cut out the slices with a round cake-cutter; this greatly improves their appearance. Pour sweet wine sauce over while hot, and serve at once.

Rhubarb Fritters.

Ingredients.—3 large tablespoonfuls of flour, 1 egg, ½ pint of milk, a small pinch of salt, 3 or 4 sticks of rhubarb—which should be young.

Method.—Mix the flour with the milk to a smooth batter, add the salt and egg, previously well beaten. Wipe the rhubarb with a damp cloth, and cut into pieces about two inches long; dip each piece in the batter and fry in boiling lard till of a nice light brown. Drain them on soft paper before the fire, that they may be quite free from fat, and serve piled high on a dish and strewn thickly with powdered sugar.

Rhubarb Jelly.

Ingredients.—Sufficient pink rhubarb to make 2 quarts when cut up quite small, ½ lb. loaf sugar, 1 oz. gelatine, 1 lemon.

Method.—Cut the rhubarb and put it in a jar with the sugar and ¼ of a pint of water; cover, and set it in the oven till the juice is all drawn out. Strain it and dissolve the gelatine in ½ a pint of the liquid; add the rind and juice of the lemon, boil all together for a few minutes, remove the lemon rind, and pour it into a mould previously wetted with cold water, and stand aside till firm.

Rhubarb Fool.

Ingredients.—1 dozen sticks of rhubarb, 2 tablespoonfuls of moist sugar, 1 teacup of water, 1 teacup of milk.

Method.—Cut the rhubarb in small pieces, add the sugar and water, and place it in a covered jar in the oven till the juice is drawn out; beat to a pulp and press it all through a sieve, stir in the milk, and set aside till cold. Serve in a glass dish.

Rhubarb Méringue Tarts.

Ingredients.—Pastry, 3 or 4 sticks of rhubarb, grated rind of a lemon, 2 eggs—whites and yolks separate; ¼ lb. of moist sugar, 3 tablespoonfuls of pounded white sugar, flavouring of vanilla—if liked.

Method.—Peel and cut the rhubarb into pieces about an inch long, put it into a covered jar with a very little water, and set it in the oven till the juice is drawn out, then add the yolks of the eggs, well beaten, the lemon rind and sugar. If the rhubarb is very juicy, some of the juice must be poured off. Line two open tart-tins with good pastry, fill with the rhubarb, and bake till of a delicate brown. Whip the whites of the eggs to a stiff froth, add the sugar and flavouring, and as soon as the tarts are done pile this *méringue* lightly upon them, and replace in the oven to slightly colour.

Rhubarb Méringue Pie.

This may be made in the same way as the tarts, only substituting a pie-dish for the tart-tins, using a little more rhubarb and *all* the juice. The red rhubarb is the nicest for both these recipes.

Moulded Rice.

Ingredients.—1 quart of milk, 6 oz. best rice, 3 oz. sugar, few drops of vanilla.

Method.—Simmer the rice in the milk for an hour-and-a-half or till quite tender, stirring frequently to prevent it burning. When done, add the sugar and flavouring, and put it into a mould previously wetted with cold water. Turn out when cold, and serve with a dish of stewed fruit, or garnish with apple jelly.

Ground Rice Pudding (Boiled).

Ingredients.—Rather more than a pint of milk, 2 or 3 bay-leaves, 2 tablespoonfuls of ground rice, sugar to taste, a small piece of butter, 3 eggs, a few drops of essence of almond.

Method.—Boil the bay-leaves in a pint of the milk, remove them and sweeten to taste. Mix the ground rice with a little cold milk, and stir it into the boiling milk for four minutes. Stand aside till nearly cold, then add a small piece of butter, the eggs well beaten, and a few drops of essence of almonds. Beat all well together, and boil in a well-buttered mould or basin from one-and-a-half to two hours. Serve with wine sauce if liked.

Rice Cheesecakes.

Ingredients.—2 eggs, ¼ lb. butter, ¼ lb. sugar, ¼ lb. ground rice, a few drops of essence of lemon.

Method.—Well whisk the eggs and add to them all the other ingredients. Line some patty-tins with pastry, fill with the mixture, and bake for about a quarter-of-an-hour.

Rice Méringue.

Ingredients.—4 oz. Carolina rice, 1¼ pints of milk, 1½ oz. butter, 3 oz. pounded white sugar, a grain or two of salt, grated rind of a small lemon, 4 large, or 5 small, eggs, whites and yolks separate, 3 tablespoonfuls of white pounded sugar for the *méringue.*

Method.—Swell the rice in the milk over a gentle fire till it is quite soft, taking care that it does not burn; stand it aside till cool, *not cold*, then add the butter, sugar, salt, lemon rind, and yolks of the eggs well beaten. Pour the mixture into a well-buttered pie-dish, and lay very lightly and equally over the top (with a tablespoon) a *méringue* made of the whites of the eggs, beaten to a stiff froth, as for sponge cakes, and mix instantly with from 3 to 4 heaped tablespoonfuls of sifted white sugar. Bake for half-an-hour in a moderate oven, but do not allow the *méringue* to colour too deeply; it should be of a clear light brown and very crisp. Serve either hot or cold, as preferred. 2 oz. Jordan almonds, with 2 or 3 bitter ones, pounded to a paste, will improve this dish, mixed with the pudding itself, or with the *méringue*, but it is exceedingly good without them.

Note.—Half the above quantity is enough for a small pudding.

Rice Flummery.

Ingredients.—¼ lb. rice flour, rather more than a pint of milk, sugar to taste, flavouring of cinnamon and lemon.

Method.—Mix the rice flour with a little cold milk, pour on to it a pint of boiling milk, which has been flavoured with cinnamon and the peel of a lemon; sweeten to taste with loaf sugar. Gently boil until it thickens, stirring all the time; put it into a mould till cold; serve on a glass dish, and ornament round with raspberry preserve.

Rhenish Cream.

Ingredients.—1 oz. gelatine, soaked in cold water, pint of boiling water, yolks of six eggs, juice and *thin* rind of two lemons, ½ pint of sherry or other light wine, sugar to taste.

Method.—Pour the boiling water on to the soaked gelatine; beat the yolks of the eggs, add the lemon rind and juice, then the wine and sugar; stir the whole into the gelatine and water, gently boil until it thickens; strain into a basin; stir till nearly cold before putting it into the mould.

Solid Custard.

Ingredients.—1 quart of milk, thin rind of 1 lemon, 7 oz. sugar, 1 oz. gelatine, yolks of 4 eggs, well beaten, 15 bitter almonds, 11 sweet almonds—blanched and chopped very fine.

Method.—Simmer the milk with the lemon rind and sugar, remove the rind, and pour the boiling milk on the gelatine, which should be soaked in cold water; add the yolks of the eggs and the almonds, gently boil for five minutes, pour into a mould, and stand aside till quite cold.

Snow Pudding.

Ingredients.—1 pint milk, 3 ozs. breadcrumbs, the grated rind of a lemon, the yolks of 3 eggs, ½ oz. butter, sugar to taste.

Method.—Cover the bottom of the dish with any kind of preserve, pour the mixture over it and bake an hour. Beat the whites of the eggs and a little sifted sugar into a stiff froth just before taking it out of the oven, and pour over; put it into the oven for a few minutes to brown. This pudding is best cold.

Snow-drift Pudding.

Ingredients.—½ ounce of gelatine soaked in cold water, ½ pint of water, ½ pound of white sugar, the juice of 4 lemons, and whites of 2 eggs.

Method.—Dissolve the gelatine in the water, add the sugar and juice, and boil about ten minutes. Strain it and let it stand still cold, and it begins to thicken, then add the whites of the eggs well beaten, and whisk briskly till it is very light and spongy; pile it in a glass dish, and set in a *very cold* place till used.

Strawberry Méringue.

Ingredients.—Puff paste, ½ pint of strawberries (good measure), sugar to taste, whites of 3 eggs, 3 tablespoonfuls of white pounded sugar for the *méringue*.

Method.—Cut a round of puff paste as large as a dinner plate, and bake to a light brown. Draw to the oven door and lay upon it the strawberries rolled in sugar, and cover these with a *méringue*, made of the whipped whites and sugar. Heap it on so as to appear as rocky as possible, and bake till it is faintly tinged with yellow brown. Serve fresh but not hot.

Sponge Cake Pudding.

Ingredients.—6 sponge cakes (*stale*), 18 small ratafias, 1 quart of milk, and 5 or 6 eggs.

Method.—Arrange the sponge cakes in a deep glass dish, with the ratafias between; pour over them about ⅓ a pint of hot milk, just enough to soak the cakes without leaving any milk in the dish; make a boiled custard with 1½ pints of milk and 5 or 6 eggs, and a little sugar. When cool enough, pour this over the cakes, grate a little nutmeg on the top, and stand aside till cold.

Sponge Custard.

Ingredients.—1 pint of milk, yolks of two eggs, white of one, if large, ½ oz. of gelatine, soaked in cold water, two tablespoonfuls of white sifted sugar, flavour to taste with vanilla.

Method.—Heat the milk and stir into the well-beaten *yolks* and sugar, return it to the saucepan, and stir till it thickens. Melt the soaked gelatine by adding a tablespoonful of boiling water, and setting it in a vessel of hot water; when it is quite melted, add it to the milk; when well mixed, flavour and set by to cool. As soon as it begins to congeal, whisk it thoroughly with an egg-beater, and add to it gradually the white of an egg previously whipped to a stiff froth. Beat it rapidly and thoroughly till quite spongy, and fill up a mould. Set in a cold place till quite firm, five or six hours at least. Dip the mould in hot water to loosen the pudding when you are ready for it, and serve on a glass dish. The above quantities will fill a quart mould. It can be made the day before it is required if convenient to do so.

St. Thomas' Pudding.

Ingredients.—3 large tablespoonfuls of flour, 1 pint of boiling milk, a little cold milk, grated rind of a lemon, yolks of 4 eggs, whites of 2 eggs, 1 good tablespoonful of castor sugar, a few raisins, and a little candied peel.

Method.—Mix the flour to a smooth paste with a little cold milk, and pour upon it the pint of boiling milk, stirring all the time. Add the lemon rind, the eggs (which should first be well beaten), and the sugar. Line a buttered mould with a few stoned raisins and some slices of candied peel, fill up with the pudding, tie a cloth over, and steam for two hours. Let it stand for five minutes before turning out, and serve with arrowroot or wine sauce.

Teacup Plum Pudding.

Ingredients.—A teacup each of raisins, currants, sugar, flour, suet, and breadcrumbs; a pinch of salt, and 2 eggs (well beaten), a little milk, to make the pudding of the right consistency.

Method.—Stone the raisins, wash and dry the currants, chop the suet quite fine, mix all the dry ingredients well together, and bind with the eggs and milk, and flavour with lemon, nutmeg, or brandy to taste. Boil for three hours; serve with wine sauce, if liked.

Third Buffs Pudding.

Ingredients.—1 pint of milk, 3 tablespoonfuls of flour, 2 oz. of butter, 6 lumps of sugar, 1 lemon rind (grated fine), 3 eggs, a small pinch of salt.

Method.—Mix the flour in the milk by degrees and boil until quite thick, stirring all the time. Take it off the fire, stir in the butter, sugar, and lemon rind, let it stand till cold, then beat in the eggs. Line a pie-dish with paste, pour in the mixture, and bake in a slow oven for one hour. If liked, spread marmalade over the top before sending to table; but it should be served as soon as possible when done. *Sufficient for a large pudding.*

Uncle Toby's Pudding.

Ingredients.—½ pint of milk, 4 laurel leaves, 8 oz. breadcrumbs, 3 oz. butter, 3 oz. white sugar, a little grated nutmeg and lemon peel, 2 eggs (well beaten), a glass of white wine.

Method.—Boil the laurel leaves in the milk, and pour it boiling on to the breadcrumbs, butter, sugar, lemon peel, and nutmeg. Beat until quite cold; then add the eggs and wine. Continue to beat until it is ready for the oven, and bake for half-an-hour.

The Welcome Guest Pudding.

Ingredients.—8 oz. breadcrumbs, ½ pint of milk, 4 oz. suet, 3 oz. ratafias, 3 oz. of candied peel, 1 lemon rind, 4 eggs, 4 oz. of white sugar, and pinch of salt.

Method.—Pour, quite boiling, on 4 oz. of breadcrumbs, an exact ½ pint of milk, set a plate over it, and stand aside till quite cold; then stir into it 4 oz. dry breadcrumbs, the finely-chopped suet, a pinch of salt, the coarsely-crushed ratifias, the candied citron and orange peel, sliced thin, and the grated rind of a large lemon. Clear and well whisk 4 large eggs, add to them by degrees 4 oz. white sifted sugar, and whisk until it is dissolved; beat them into the other ingredients, and when well mixed, pour it into a thickly-buttered mould or basin, which will hold a quart. The mixture should fill it within half-an-inch of the top. First cover with a buttered paper, then a floured cloth; tie these down very securely, and boil for two hours at the utmost. Let it stand a minute or two before turning it out, and serve with simple wine sauce. In summer 1 lb. of fresh fruit, stewed with $\frac{1}{2}$ a lb. of white sugar, is a good substitute for the wine sauce.

CAKES.

A Plain Cake.

Ingredients.—½ lb. of good beef dripping (clarified), 1½ lb. flour, ¼ lb. sugar, ½ oz. caraway seeds, 1 pint of milk, 1 tablespoonful of carbonate of soda.

Method.—Rub the dripping into the flour, add the sugar and caraway seeds, and mix all together with the milk, in which the soda has been dissolved. Bake at once for 1½ hours.

Biscuits.

Ingredients.—½ lb. flour, ¼ lb. pounded white sugar, 3 oz. butter, ½ teaspoonful of carbonate of ammonia, a few drops of essence of lemon, yolks of 2 eggs, white of 1 egg.

Method.—Mix the dry ingredients well together, taking care that there are no lumps in the ammonia, then add the well-whisked eggs; roll out, cut into biscuits not very small, and bake in a brisk oven.

Christmas Cake.

Ingredients.—1 lb. flour, ½ lb. currants, ½ lb. butter, ¼ lb. sugar, 2 oz. lemon peel, 2 teaspoonfuls baking powder, 3 eggs, ½ pint of milk.

Method.—Mix the baking powder thoroughly in the flour, then rub in the butter, add the sugar, currants, and lemon peel, beat the eggs and mix them with the milk, and after mixing them all thoroughly together bake in a papered tin in a moderate oven.

Gingerbread Loaf.

Ingredients.—Butter, treacle, and sugar, 1 teacupful of each; ½ a teacup of cold water, 1 tablespoonful of ground ginger; soda dissolved in water, and cinnamon, 1 teaspoonful of each; flour to make a stiff batter.

Method.—Melt the butter, slightly warm the treacle, sugar, and spice, and beat together for ten minutes; then add the water, soda, and flour. Stir well, make into three small loaves, and bake in a moderate oven.

Whole Wheat Meal Gingerbread.

Ingredients.—1¼ lb. wheat meal, 1 lb. treacle, ¼ lb. sugar, ¼ lb. butter, ¾ oz. caraway seeds bruised,

¾ oz. ginger, ¼ oz. lemon peel, ½ pint of new milk, 1 teaspoonful of soda.

Method.—Mix the dry ingredients, then add the treacle and milk, in which the soda should be dissolved. Bake in a buttered tin in a very slow oven.

Plain Gingerbread Cakes.

Ingredients.—1 lb. of flour, 6 oz. butter, or good beef dripping, 1 oz. ground ginger, 4 oz. brown sugar, ½ teaspoonful of cloves and mace, pounded, ¾ lb. treacle, grated lemon or candied peel, if liked.

Method.—Work the butter or dripping into the flour, then add the ginger, sugar, cloves, and mace; next add ¾ lb. of treacle, or rather more if necessary; roll out the paste, cut with a round cake-cutter, and bake on a floured tin in a slow oven.

Lunch Cake.

Ingredients.—1¼ lb. flour, ½ lb. currants, ½ lb. sugar, 6 oz. butter, 3 eggs, 4 teaspoonfuls of baking powder, 6 drops essence of lemon (or small quantity of grated nutmeg), a teacupful of milk.

Method.—First well mix all the dry ingredients, lastly adding the eggs and milk; beat well for a few minutes, and bake at once. Sufficient for *two* medium-sized cakes.

Madeira Cake.

Ingredients.—¼ lb. flour, 1 teaspoonful of baking powder, 2½ oz. butter, 2½ oz. sugar, 2 eggs.

Method.—Cream the butter, add the sugar, then the flour, with which the baking powder has been mixed. Lastly, add the well-beaten eggs, and bake in a buttered tin for half-an-hour.

Orange Cake (*In layers*).

Ingredients.—3 oz. butter, 3 oz. white pounded sugar, 1 teacup of milk, 2 eggs, flavour to taste, 5 oz. flour.

Method.—Beat the butter to a cream, add the sugar, then the milk and *yolks* of the eggs, well beaten, dredge in the flour by degrees, beat well, and, lastly, add the *whites* of the eggs, previously well whisked. Spread the mixture equally on the centre part of *three* dinner-plates, well buttered, so as to obtain three cakes of equal size, and bake in a quick oven to a delicate brown. Stand them aside till cool.

MIXTURE FOR FILLING.

Ingredients.—1 lemon, 2 oranges, 1 teacup of sugar, 1 teacup of water, 1 tablespoonful of cornflour.

Method.—Grate the yellow part of the rind of the oranges and lemon, and strain the juice; wet the cornflour with the water, mix in the sugar, and add this to the rind and juice; boil for a few minutes, stirring all the time, then let it get quite cool. Place one of the cakes—which should be cool, not quite cold, or it may break—on the dish in which it is to be served, spread it with *half* the mixture; place a second cake on the top, spread over the rest of the mixture, and place the third cake above; gently press them together, and sprinkle a little white sugar over the top. The filling should be made first, to be ready for the cakes.

Oswego Sponge Cakes.

Ingredients.—8 oz. cornflour, 6 oz. white sugar, bruised, 4 oz. butter, 3 eggs, 1 teaspoonful baking powder.

Method.—Beat all well together; bake in small tins in a slow oven.

Pound Cakes.

Ingredients.—½ lb. flour, ½ lb. butter, ½ lb. white pounded sugar, 4 eggs, peel if liked.

Method.—Beat the butter to a cream, taking care

to beat it all one way, add the sugar and flour, and lastly the eggs—well beaten. Beat the mixture for twenty minutes. Cover the sides and bottom of a cake-tin with well buttered paper, pour in the mixture, and bake in a moderate oven.

Queen's Buns.

Ingredients.—4 eggs, the weight of the eggs in flour and sugar, the weight of three eggs in butter, 4 drops of essence of lemon, ½ teaspoonful of baking powder, a few currants, if liked,

Method.—Beat the butter and eggs to a cream, add the sugar and beat again well, add the essence, and lastly stir in the flour. Bake in tins for about a quarter-of-an-hour in a brisk oven, having strewed a few currants on the top of each bun before baking.

Rice Cakes.

Ingredients.—¼ lb. ground rice, 2 oz. butter, 2 oz. pounded white sugar, 1 egg.

Method.—Beat the butter to a cream, stir in the rice and sugar and moisten with the egg, which should be well beaten. Roll out the paste, cut with a small round pastry-cutter, and bake in a very *slow* oven from eighteen to twenty minutes.

Rice Cake:

Ingredients.—½ lb. ground rice, ½ lb. sugar, 20 drops of essence of lemon, 4 eggs, ¼ lb. of butter.

Method.—Beat the eggs well, whites and yolks separately, add them to the other ingredients, and beat for half-an-hour. Bake in a tin lined with buttered paper.

Rice Buns.

Ingredients.—4 eggs, 3 oz. butter, ½ lb. pounded loaf sugar, ¼ lb. ground rice, ¼ lb. flour, 1 small teaspoonful of powdered ammonia.

Method.—Cream the butter, add the sugar, flour, rice, and ammonia, and, lastly, the whisked eggs. Bake at once in small tins, in a moderate oven. This quantity makes two dozen buns. They should be only a little darker than sponge cakes when baked.

Rusks.

Ingredients.—1 lb. of flour, 3 oz. butter, 3 oz. lard, 2 teaspoonfuls of baking powder, 1 teaspoonful of sugar, ½ teaspoonful of salt, 2 eggs, as much milk as necessary to make into a stiff paste.

Method.—Mix with the flour the baking powder,

sugar, and salt; rub in the butter and lard. Well beat the eggs, and add about a tablespoonful of milk; pour this into the middle of the flour, and mix with a fork. Roll out once only, till about half-an-inch thick, cut with a round cutter, and bake on a tin *at once*. When partly done, split each in half with a fork, and put back into the oven until slightly brown and crisp.

Soda Cake.

Ingredients.—1 lb. of flour, ½ lb. sugar, ½ lb. butter, ¾ lb. currants, ½ oz. of candied peel, 1 teaspoonful of carbonate of soda, 1 pint of milk, 3 eggs.

Method.—Rub the butter into the flour, add the other dry ingredients, and, lastly, the milk and well-whisked eggs. Bake in two buttered cake-tins, in a moderate oven.

Soda Buns.

Ingredients.—½ lb. of flour, 3 oz. of butter, 4 oz. of sugar, a little candied peel, 1 oz. of currants, a pinch of salt, a teacupful of milk, ½ a small teaspoonful of carbonate of soda, yolks of 2 eggs, and the white of 1.

Method.—Rub the butter well into the flour, add

the sugar, currants, and peel, pour the milk on boiling, and add the beaten eggs; when well mixed, dust over and stir well in the carbonate of soda, which should be well powdered. Bake in buttered patty-tins until firm to the touch and coloured underneath. They need not be baked immediately.

Scotch Shortbread.

Ingredients.—2 lb. flour, ½ lb. powdered loaf sugar, ½ lb. currants (if liked), 6 oz. candied peel (cut fine), 10 oz. butter, 6 oz. lard, ½ teaspoonful carbonate of soda, 1 tablespoonful water.

Method.—Mix all the dry ingredients together. Soften the lard and butter together in a lined saucepan, with the water, and when it has cooled again and is of the consistence of batter, mix it with the other ingredients, to form a rather stiff dough. Divide it into eight equal pieces, and work out each piece with the hand into a flat, round cake, not more than half-an-inch thick, and, as nearly as possible, the same size. Pinch them round the edges with the finger and thumb, cut a small round out of the centre, and the rest of the cake into six or eight pieces. Bake on flat tins, covered with paper, from three-quarters of an hour to an hour. They should be a very pale, delicate colour when done. The pieces will need to be parted again with a knife, as they join while baking. When perfectly cold, pile on two plates, with castor sugar sifted between each layer.

Sponge Cake.

Ingredients.—¾ lb. powdered loaf sugar, ½ lb. flour, ¼ pint water, the yolks of 8 eggs, the whites of 4.

Method.—First prepare the tins in the following manner:—Take two medium-sized cake-tins, warm them, then lard the insides *very thoroughly*. When the tins are cool, sprinkle the insides all over with finely-powdered loaf sugar; then gently shake out all that may be loose in the tins. This mode of preparation forms a nice delicate crust outside the cakes. Now set the flour to warm in front of the fire, occasionally turning it over to ensure all being well dried. Boil the sugar and water together in a lined saucepan, and when thoroughly dissolved pour the boiling mixture on the eggs, which should be previously whisked a few times. Beat this mixture three-quarters of an hour; then gradually stir in the flour. taking care that no knots remain in the cake. Do not beat it more than is necessary to well mix in the flour. Then pour quickly into the tins, which should be about half filled; bake from three-quarters of an hour to an hour in a medium oven, taking care not to let them brown too quickly.

They may be tried with a clean skewer. If nothing adheres to it when it is withdrawn, the cakes are done, and may be turned out to cool on a wire sieve. Half this quantity will make a nice cake.

Sly Cakes.

Ingredients.—1 lb. of flour, 8 oz. butter, 8 oz. currants, 2 oz. sugar, and 6 drops of essence of lemon.

Method.—Mix the flour and sugar, and make it into a smooth paste with water, but do not make it very wet. Roll out three times, and spread in the butter as for pastry. Roll it very thin, and cut into round or square cakes. Spread half of them very thickly with currants, press the others gently on the top, so as to form a sandwich, and bake in a quick oven till of a light brown. If preferred, jam may be used instead of the currants.

Seed Cake.

Ingredients.—1½ lb. of flour, ¼ lb. butter, ¼ lb. lard, 1 oz. caraway seeds, ½ lb. sifted sugar, a pinch of salt, 2 eggs, ¾ of a pint of milk, 2 drachms of carbonate of soda, 1½ drachm tartaric acid.

Method.—Mix the dry ingredients well together;

then add the milk and eggs, which should be previously well beaten. Bake at once in a moderate oven.

Scones.

Ingredients.—1 lb. flour, ¼ lb. butter, ½ small teaspoonful salt, ¼ teaspoonful of soda, ¼ teaspoonful tartaric acid.

Method.—Mix with milk, and roll out half-an-inch thick, cut with a tumbler, and bake about fifteen or twenty minutes.

Tea Cakes.—No. 1.

Ingredients.—1 lb. of flour, 2 oz. butter, 1½ teaspoonfuls of baking powder, 1 egg, 2 teaspoonfuls of sugar, and a few currants.

Method.—Mix all together with a little cold milk, make into small cakes, and bake at once in a quick oven.

Tea Cakes.—No. 2.

Ingredients.—2 lbs. of flour, 1 small teaspoonful of salt, 2 tablespoonfuls of white sugar, 2 oz. butter, 2 oz. lard, 1 egg, ½ oz. of German yeast, warm milk or water about ⅔ a pint

Method.—Put the yeast into a little of the warm —*not hot*—milk or water, and stand it in a warm place for a few minutes to rise. See that the flour is quite dry, and well mix with it the sugar and salt, then rub in the butter and lard. Well beat the egg, stir it into the yeast—which should be strained—and mix these with the flour, adding as much warm milk or water as will make it into a smooth paste; knead it well, cover with a cloth, and set near the fire for about half-an-hour, till it has well risen; then form into round cakes, place them on tins, let them rise again before putting into the oven, and bake in a moderate heat from fifteen to thirty minutes. When partly cooked, draw them to the oven door, and brush over with a little milk and sprinkle with sugar, then close the oven till they are done. Cut in slices, toast and butter them for the table.

Note.—All the sugar may be omitted from this recipe if quite plain cakes are desired.

Victoria Buns.

Ingredients.—1 egg and its weight in flour, 2 oz. pounded loaf sugar, 1½ oz. ground rice, 2 oz. butter, 1½ oz. currants, a few thin slices of peel.

Method.—Whisk the egg, stir in the sugar, and beat these ingredients well together. Beat the butter to a cream, stir in the ground rice, currants, and peel, and after adding the egg, stir in a little flour; but do not make them very stiff. Bake in small patty-tins for about a quarter-of-an-hour.

White Cake.

Ingredients.—Whites of 3 eggs, 1 teacup of white sugar, 1 teacup of flour, 1 teacup of cornflour, ½ teacup of butter, ½ teacup of milk, 2 spoonfuls of baking powder, flavour to taste. Lemon is best.

Method.—Beat the butter to a cream, add the sugar and other ingredients, and lastly the eggs (whites only), well beaten. Bake at once in a moderate oven.

Yorkshire Cake.

Ingredients.—1 egg, its weight in flour, butter, ground rice, and sugar; 1 teaspoonful of baking powder, and a very little milk.

Method.—Mix all together, spread over two dessert-plates, well buttered, and bake from ten to fifteen minutes. When finished, slip them off the plates, spread preserve upon one, and press the second cake gently on the top; then sprinkle with castor sugar.

EGGS.

Eggs sur le Plat.

Ingredients.—6 eggs, 1 tablespoonful of butter or nice dripping. Pepper and salt to taste.

Method.—Melt the butter on a stone-china or tin plate, or shallow baking-dish. Break the eggs carefully into this; dust lightly with pepper and salt, and put in a moderate oven until the whites are well "set." Serve in the dish in which they were baked.

Toasted Eggs.

Ingredients.—Round of toast, eggs, 1 slice of fat pork.

Method.—Cover the bottom of an earthenware or stone-china dish with rounds of delicately toasted bread. Or, what is even better, with rounds of stale bread dipped in beaten egg and fried quickly in butter or nice dripping, to a golden brown. Break an egg carefully upon each, and set the dish immediately in front of and on a level with a glowing fire. Toast over this a slice of fat corned pork or ham, holding it so that it will toast very quickly, and all the dripping fall upon the eggs. When these are well "set," and a crust begins to form upon the top of each, they are done. Turn the dish several times while toasting the meat, that the eggs may be equally cooked. Do not send the pork to table, but pepper the eggs lightly and remove with the toast to the dish in which they are to go to the table, with a cake-turner or flat ladle, taking care not to break them.

Baked Eggs.—No. 1.

Ingredients.—6 eggs, 4 tablespoonfuls good gravy —veal, beef or poultry, the latter is particularly nice—1 handful breadcrumbs, 6 rounds buttered toast or fried bread.

Method.—Put the gravy into a shallow baking-dish. Break the eggs into this, pepper and salt them, and strew the breadcrumbs over them. Bake for five minutes in a quick oven. Take up the eggs carefully one by one, and lay upon the toast, which must be arranged on a hot flat dish. Add a little cream, and, if you like, some very-finely chopped parsley and onion, to the gravy left in the baking-dish, and turn it into a saucepan. Boil up once quickly, and pour over the eggs.

Baked Eggs.—No. 2.

Ingredients.—6 eggs, 1 cup of chicken, game, or veal gravy, 1 teaspoonful mixed parsley and onion chopped fine, 1 handful very fine breadcrumbs, pepper and salt to taste.

Method.—Pour enough gravy into a neat baking-dish to cover the bottom well, and mix with the rest the parsley and onion, set the dish in the oven until the gravy begins to hiss and bubble, when break the eggs into it, so that they do not crowd one another. Strew breadcrumbs thickly over them, pepper and salt, and return to the oven for three minutes longer. Then pour the rest of the gravy, which should be hot, over the whole. More breadcrumbs, as fine as dust, and bake until the eggs are "set." Send to table in the baking-dish. This dish will be found very savoury.

Fricasseed Eggs.

Ingredients.—6 hard-boiled eggs (when cold, slice with a sharp knife, taking care not to break the yolk), 1 cup good broth, well seasoned with pepper and salt, parsley, and a suspicion of onion, some rounds stale bread, fried to a light brown in butter or nice dripping.

Method.—Put the broth on the fire in a saucepan

with the seasoning, and let it come to a boil. Rub the slices of egg with melted butter, then roll them in flour. Lay them gently in the gravy, and let this become smoking hot upon the side of the range, but do not let it actually boil, lest the eggs should break. They should lie thus in the gravy for at least five minutes. Have ready, upon a flat dish, the fried bread. Lay the sliced egg evenly upon this, pour the gravy over all, and serve hot.

Egg Cutlets.

Ingredients.—6 hard-boiled eggs, 1 raw egg well beaten, 1 handful very fine dry breadcrumbs, pepper and salt, and a little parsley minced fine, 3 tablespoonfuls butter or dripping, 1 cup broth or drawn butter, in which a raw egg has been beaten.

Method.—Cut the boiled eggs, when perfectly cold, into rather thick slices with a sharp, thin knife, dip each slice into the beaten egg, roll in the breadcrumbs, which should be seasoned with pepper, salt, and minced parsley. Fry them to a light brown in the butter or dripping, turning each piece as it is done on the under side. Do not let them lie in the frying-pan an instant after they are cooked. Drain free from fat before laying them on a hot dish. Pour the gravy, boiling hot, over the eggs, and send to table.

Potted Eggs.

Ingredients.—The yolks of 6 hard-boiled eggs, 1 ounce of butter, 1 teaspoonful of anchovy sauce, a little salt and cayenne pepper.

Method.—Pound the eggs and butter well together in a mortar, then add the salt and cayenne pepper, and lastly the anchovy sauce. Must be used within a few days.

Stirred Eggs.

Ingredients.—6 eggs, 3 tablespoonfuls of gravy, that made from poultry is best. Enough fried toast, from which the crust has been pared, to cover the bottom of a flat dish, a very little anchovy paste, 1 tablespoonful of butter.

Method.—Melt the butter in a frying-pan, and when hot break into this the eggs; stir in the gravy, pepper and salt to taste, and continue to stir very quickly, and well up from the bottom, for about two minutes, or until the whole is a soft, yellow mass. Have ready in a flat dish the fried toast, spread thinly with anchovy paste. Heap the stirred egg upon this, and serve before it has time to harden.

Scalloped Eggs.

Ingredients.—6 eggs boiled hard, and when cold cut into thin slices, 1 cupful fine breadcrumbs, well moistened with a little good gravy, and a little milk, ½ cup thick melted butter, into which has been beaten the yolk of an egg, 1 small cupful minced ham, tongue, poultry, or cold halibut, salmon, or cod. Pepper and salt to taste.

Method.—Put a layer of moistened crumbs in the bottom of a buttered baking-dish; on this lay the sliced eggs, each piece of which must have been dipped in the thick melted butter. Sprinkle the ground meat over these, cover with another layer of breadcrumbs, and proceed in like manner until the egg is all used up. Sift on the top a good layer of dry breadcrumbs. Cover the dish with an inverted plate until the contents are heated through, then remove the plate and brown the top upon the upper grating of the oven.

Whirled Eggs.

Ingredients.—6 eggs, 1 quart boiling water, some thin slices of buttered toast, pepper and salt to taste, a tablespoonful of butter.

Method.—Put the water, slightly salted, in a saucepan over the fire, and keep it at a fast boil.

Stir with a wooden spoon or ladle in one direction until it whirls rapidly. Break the eggs, one at a time, into a cup, and drop each carefully into the centre or vortex of the boiling whirlpool, which must be kept in rapid motion until the egg is a soft, round ball. Take it out carefully with a perforated spoon, and put it on a slice of buttered toast laid upon a hot dish. Put a bit of butter on the top, set the dish in the oven to keep it warm, and proceed in the same way with each egg, having but one at a time in the saucepan. When all are done, dust lightly with salt and pepper, and send up hot.

Eggs Poached with Mushrooms.

Ingredients.—6 eggs, 1 teacupful of cold chicken or other fowl minced fine, 2 tablespoonfuls of butter, about a cupful of good gravy (veal or poultry), 2 dozen mushrooms of fair size, sliced, some rounds of fried bread, 1 raw egg beaten light.

Method.—Mince the cold meat very fine and work into it the butter with the beaten egg. Season with pepper and salt, and stir it over the fire in a sauce pan until it is smoking hot. Poach the eggs, and trim off the ragged edges. The fried bread must be arranged upon a hot flat dish, the mince of chicken on this, and the eggs upon the chicken. Have ready in another saucepan the sliced mushrooms and gravy. If you use the French *champignons*—tinned—they should have simmered in the gravy fifteen minutes; if fresh ones, you should have parboiled them in clean water as long, before they are sliced into the gravy, and stewed ten minutes in it. The gravy must be savoury, rich, and rather highly seasoned. Pour it very hot upon the eggs.

ODDS AND ENDS.

Cheese Fingers.

Ingredients.—3 oz. grated cheese, 3 oz. flour, 2 oz. butter, ½ teaspoonful of baking powder, salt and cayenne to taste.

Method.—Mix these ingredients to a stiff paste with a very little milk, roll out and cut into strips about three inches long, roll round, and bake on a tin in a brisk oven for five minutes, to a very light brown. This is a good way to use up dry pieces of cheese, and makes a pretty dish for the table.

Cheese Biscuits.

Ingredients.—Pastry, grated cheese, pepper and salt, cayenne if liked.

Method.—Roll the pastry out thin, strew grated cheese, seasoned, over the whole sheet, and roll up tightly. Roll out again, even thinner than before, and strew upon it the rest of the cheese. Roll up again, and set in a cold place for half-an-hour, to get crisp. Roll out again into a sheet, cut into any fanciful shapes, prick with a fork, and bake very quickly in a hot oven. Brush over with beaten egg while hot, strew fine raspings of cheese over the top, and close the oven for an instant to glaze the biscuits. Serve hot or cold.

Cheese Pâtés.

Ingredients.—Rounds of bread (cut and fried), 5 tablespoonfuls of grated cheese, ½ teacup of hot water, 1 egg (white and yolk separate), pepper and salt, ½ teacup of breadcrumbs (fine), 1 tablespoonful of butter.

Method.—Cut rather thick slices of stale bread (baker's bread is best for this purpose) into rounds with a cake-cutter. With a smaller cutter extract a piece from the middle of each round, taking care not to let the sharp edge go quite through the bread, but leaving enough in the cavity to serve as a bottom to the pâté. Dip the hollowed pieces of bread in the white of the egg, strew them with breadcrumbs, and fry in dripping or lard to a delicate brown. Drain the fat from them, and fill with the mixture made as follows:—Boil ½ cup of water, and stir in the butter, seasoning, and cheese, and when this is melted, the yolk of the egg. Heat together one minute, then stir in the breadcrumbs, and it is ready. Put a good spoonful into each pâté, brown quickly in the oven, and serve hot on a folded napkin.

Cheese Fondu.

Ingredients.—½ a teacup of breadcrumbs (very fine and dry), 1 scant cup of milk (quite fresh), ¼ lb. of old dry cheese (grated), 1 large egg (whipped very light, yolk and white separate), 1 dessert-spoonful of melted butter, pepper and salt, a pinch of soda dissolved in hot water and stirred into the milk.

Method.—Soak the crumbs in the milk, beat into these the egg, butter, seasoning, and, lastly, the cheese. Butter a shallow pie-dish, pour the *fondu* into it, strew dry breadcrumbs on the top, and bake in a rather quick oven till delicately browned. Serve at once in the dish in which it is baked, as it soon falls.

Cheese Sandwiches.

Ingredients.—¼ lb. good cheese (grated), 3 eggs (boiled hard—use the yolks only), 1 tablespoonful melted butter, 3 slices of buttered bread, pepper and salt.

Method.—Rub the yolks to a smooth paste with the butter, season, and work in the cheese. Spread the bread, and fold upon the mixture.

Lemon Syrup.

Ingredients.—4 lbs. loaf sugar, 2½ oz. tartaric acid, 2 drachms essence of lemon, 1 quart of water, boiling.

Method.—Put the sugar in a basin and pour the boiling water upon it. When dissolved and quite cool, add the essence of lemon and tartaric acid, and bottle for use. One tablespoonful to a tumbler of water makes excellent lemonade.

Horseradish Sauce.

Ingredients.—1 stick of horseradish, a teaspoonful of mustard, a little salt, ¼ pint of cream, vinegar to taste.

Method.—Grate the horseradish into a basin, add the mustard, salt, cream, and vinegar, stir all well together, and serve in a pickle-jar with roast beef.

Four Ways of Using Crusts:

1. *Bread Pudding.*—A pint of crumbs as fine as can be broken or chipped with a knife to a quart of milk, a teacup of sugar, 2 eggs, and flavouring or raisins. Cover the top, after baking, with jelly or any stewed fruit; beat the whites of the eggs and spread over, return to the oven a few moments until a light brown, and the pudding rises to the height of elegance.

2. *Dressing for Fowls or Roast of Veal.*—Chop the bread fine with a bit of butter or salt pork, one onion, salt and pepper, a pinch of sage. If the crusts are very hard, pour over them a little boiling water and pour off immediately.

3. *Macaroni Cheese.*—This dish is very much improved by layers of crumbs between the cheese and macaroni and all over the top. It absorbs the milk, and prevents it being watery, as it is sure to be without it.

4.—In making pancakes of any kind, break the crusts in bits, pour over them boiling water, and let them soak five minutes; by this time they are soft and pulpy. Drain off the water, mash fine, and stir into the batter. It is surprising how this lightens the cakes, without being seen after they are browned.

Recipes for Baking Powder.

(1) *Ingredients.*—¼ lb. ground rice, ¼ lb. carbonate of soda, 3 oz. tartaric acid, 2 oz. ammonia (pounded); mix well together.

(2) *Ingredients.*—1 lb. flour, 1 lb. carbonate of soda, ¾ lb. tartaric acid, pound well together. Keep in a close tin or well-stoppered bottle, and in a *dry* place.

Fried Apples.

Ingredients.—3 or 4 large juicy apples, butter or lard for frying.

Method.—Pare the apples and cut into rounds about ¼ of an inch thick, carefully remove the core, without breaking the apples, and fry quickly in boiling fat to a light brown. Drain free from fat, and serve *very hot* with rump steak.

Fried Cucumbers.

Ingredients.—Cucumbers, pepper and salt, flour, lard or butter.

Method.—Pare and lay in ice-water half an hour, cut lengthwise into slices nearly ½ inch thick, and lay in ice-water ten minutes longer. Wipe each piece dry with a soft cloth, sprinkle with pepper and salt, and dredge with flour. Fry to a delicate brown in sweet lard or butter.

Stewed Celery.

Ingredients.—Celery, boiling water salted, ½ pint of white sauce.

Method.—Cut off all the decayed leaves and outside pieces of the celery, and well wash it. Cut each head lengthwise into quarters, and boil in sufficient water to cover it till tender—fifteen to twenty-five minutes according to the size. Put it in a vegetable dish with the white sauce poured over it, and serve sliced lemon with it, if liked.

Celery Salad.

Ingredients.—2 heads of celery, yolks of 2 hard-boiled eggs, 1 tablespoonful of oil, pepper, salt, pounded sugar, 3 or 4 tablespoonfuls of vinegar.

Method.—Trim and wash the celery and cut it into half-inch lengths, having first laid it in cold water to become crisp. Rub the yolks of the eggs to a smooth paste with the oil, add pepper, salt, and sugar, and, by degrees—a few drops at a time—the vinegar. When it is all quite smooth, pour over the celery and serve. It must not be kept standing after it is mixed or the celery will toughen.

Baked Celery.

Ingredients.—2 heads of celery, boiling water salted, ½ pint of milk, 1 oz. of butter rolled in flour, pepper and salt, 1 egg, fine breadcrumbs.

Method.—Prepare the celery as for the salad, and stew in boiling water for ten minutes; drain off the water, add the milk, butter, pepper, and salt, and simmer for three minutes after heating; then pour it into a basin to cool. Butter a shallow pie-dish, and strew the bottom with fine breadcrumbs; when the celery is cold, beat in the egg, and pour into the dish, strew breadcrumbs thickly over the top, cover and bake for twenty minutes, then remove the cover and brown.

Celery Sauce for Boiled Poultry.

Ingredients.—2 heads of celery, 1 teacupful of broth in which the chicken or turkey is boiled, 1 teacup of milk, salt and nutmeg, 1 large tablespoonful of flour, and 1 tablespoonful of butter.

Method.—Wash and trim the celery and boil in salted water till tender, drain and cut into pieces half an inch long. Thicken the broth with the flour, add the butter, salt, nutmeg, and lastly the milk. Stir and beat until smooth, put in the celery, and heat almost to boiling, stirring all the time. Serve in a tureen.

Whipped Potatoes.

Ingredients.—Good mealy potatoes, a little melted butter, milk, pepper, and salt.

Method.—Boil the potatoes till tender, and instead of mashing them in the ordinary way, whip up with a fork on a hot dish till light and dry; then whip in the melted butter, warm milk, pepper, and salt; continue whipping quickly till it becomes a creamy mass—almost like a *méringue*—then pile as lightly and irregularly as possible on a hot dish.

Potato Puff.

Ingredients.—2 breakfast-cups of cold mashed potatoes, 2 tablespoonfuls of melted butter, 2 eggs, 1 teacup of milk, salt to taste.

Method.—Stir the butter into the potatoes, and beat till of a white cream, then add the eggs whipped very light, the milk and salt; beat all well, pour into a deep dish, and bake in a quick oven till brown.

Potato Cakes.

Ingredients.—Potatoes, flour, a little milk, lard or dripping.

Method.—Make cold mashed potatoes into flat cakes (with a little milk if dry); flour and fry in lard or good sweet dripping, until they are a light brown.

Potato Scallops.

Ingredients.—Potatoes, melted butter, salt, and pepper.

Method.—Boil and mash the potatoes soft with a little milk. Beat up light with melted butter—a dessert-spoonful for every $\frac{1}{2}$ pint of potatoes—salt and pepper to taste. Fill some patty-tins or buttered scallop-shells with the mixture, and brown in an oven when you have stamped a pattern on the top of each. Glaze while hot with a little butter and serve in the shells. If liked, strew some grated cheese over the top.

Potato Chips.

Ingredients.—Potatoes, salted lard.

Method.—Peel and slice some good potatoes, and lay them in cold water for an hour. Dry by laying them upon a dry towel and pressing them with another. Fry in salted lard, quickly, to a delicate brown. Take out as soon as they are done; shake briskly in a hot colander, to free them from fat, and serve at once in a hot dish, lined with a napkin.

Potato Balls.

Ingredients.—Potatoes, milk, butter, pepper and salt.

Method.—Boil the potatoes till tender, strain and mash them with a very little milk, pepper, salt, and a bit of butter; make them into round balls with the hand, place them on a dish, and set in the oven to brown.

Parsnip Fritters.

Ingredients.—3 large parsnips, 1 egg, 1 teacup of milk, 1 tablespoonful of butter, 3 tablespoonfuls of flour, 1 teaspoonful of salt.

Method.—Boil the parsnips till quite tender, and

mash them quite smooth, picking out any woody bits. Beat the egg to a froth, stir in the mashed parsnips and beat well; add the salt and butter, then the milk, and lastly the flour. Make into round cakes or balls and fry quickly, in boiling lard or clarified dripping, to a nice brown.

Ladies' Cabbage.

Ingredients.—1 firm white cabbage, 1 large egg, 1 tablespoonful of melted butter, pepper, salt, a very little milk, fine breadcrumbs.

Method.—Boil the cabbage in two waters, and let it get quite cold; then cut it up very fine, add the butter, pepper, and salt, egg, and milk, stir all up together, and when well mixed, put it into a buttered pie-dish, strew with fine crumbs, and bake covered for half-an-hour; remove the cover, brown, and serve.

Macaroni, with Tomato Sauce.

Ingredients.—½ lb. of macaroni, 1 teacup of gravy or stock, 4 ripe tomatoes, seasoning of pepper, salt, and grated cheese, 1 oz. of butter rolled in flour.

Method.—Break the macaroni into inch lengths, and cook for twenty minutes in boiling water, salted.

Make the gravy quite hot, slice into it the tomatoes, stew till tender, then strain through net or tarlatan into a saucepan, season well, stir in the butter, and simmer for five minutes. Put the macaroni into a deep dish, sprinkling grated cheese over each layer, and pour the hot sauce over, opening the mass with a fork that it may reach the bottom layers. Serve with hot beef or mutton.

Spinach, with Egg Dressing.

Ingredients.—2 pailfuls of spinach, 1 oz. butter, pepper, salt, 1 teaspoonful of sugar, 3 hard-boiled eggs, a little milk.

Method.—Well wash the spinach in two waters that it may be quite free from grit, and cook in boiling water, salted, for twenty minutes. Strain through a colander, and chop it very fine; return it to the saucepan with the butter, pepper, salt, and sugar. Have ready the yolks of 3 hard-boiled eggs rubbed to powder and wetted with a little milk, stir all together in the saucepan with a wire spoon, till smooth and thick; turn into a vegetable dish, and garnish with the whites of the eggs cut into rings.

Spinach, with Poached Eggs.

Ingredients.—Spinach, 1 oz. butter, pepper and salt, eggs—allow one for each person.

Method.—Prepare the spinach as in the foregoing recipe, but leaving out the eggs and milk. Pile it two or three inches high on a flat dish, and lay the poached eggs on the top.

Note.—This is a nice dish for supper, especially if a few rolls of toasted bacon are laid round it.

Tomato Salad.

Ingredients.—6 large tomatoes, 1 teaspoonful of sugar, ½ teaspoonful each of salt, pepper, and made mustard, 2 tablespoonfuls of oil, the yolk of 1 egg, 5 tablespoonfuls of vinegar.

Method.—Mix the sugar, salt, pepper, and mustard with the oil, and when smooth, beat in the yolk of a raw egg; then by degrees—a few drops at a time—the vinegar. Peel and slice the tomatoes with a sharp knife, lay them in a glass dish, pour over the dressing and serve.

Baked Tomatoes.

Ingredients.—6 or 8 large ripe tomatoes, 1 slice of salt pork or ham, breadcrumbs, pepper, sugar.

Method.—Peel and slice the tomatoes, mince the pork very fine; put a layer of tomatoes in a buttered pie-dish, season with sugar and pepper, strew with breadcrumbs, and scatter a little pork over it. Fill the dish in this order, having crumbs at the top, cover closely, and bake for half-an-hour, or till the juice bubbles up at the side. Remove the cover, brown, and serve.

Note.—The pork may be omitted if preferred, but a little salt must then be used.

Apple Jelly.

Ingredients.—To each quart of juice add $1\frac{1}{2}$ lb. of loaf sugar, 1 lemon.

Method.—Pare and core 2 quarts of apples, cut them as for pies; boil the cores and parings in as much water as will cover them; strain it and put the apples into a pipkin with the liquor, set them in a slow oven, and let them stand till they are quite of a pulp. Have ready a thin linen bag to put them in, and hang up till the liquor has run from it. Put the rind of a large lemon into your basin where the liquor runs, and to one quart of juice add one pound and a-half of loaf sugar, with the juice of the lemon. Boil it gently for one hour, and pour into moulds previously dipped in cold water. If put into dry moulds or glasses and covered with paper dipped in brandy, it will keep good for a year.

Imitation Preserved Ginger.

Ingredients.—3 lb. vegetable-marrow, 3 lb. loaf sugar, 1 oz. ground ginger, rind and juice of 2 lemons.

Method.—Peel the marrow, take out the seeds, and slice into pieces about an inch thick and two or three inches long; strain the lemon juice, and cut the rind very fine; put all the ingredients into a stewpan, and boil all together till clear—about one hour. Tie down as for other preserves.

Mincemeat.

Ingredients.—2 lb. suet, 2½ lb. currants, 2 lb. raisins, 1 lb. sugar, ¼ lb. each of candied lemon, citron, and orange peel, 12 large apples, the juice of 4 lemons and peel of 2, ½ oz. salt, ½ oz. ground ginger, ½ oz. ground cloves, ½ oz. nutmegs, ½ oz.

allspice, ¼ pint of brandy (or whisky), and ½ pint of wine.

Method.—Chop the suet very fine; wash the currants, pick them free from stalks or grit, and spread them on a dish to dry; stone and cut the raisins once or twice across; slice the candied peel; pare, core, and mince the apples; mince the lemon peel and strain the juice, and grate the nutmeg. When all the ingredients are prepared, mix them well together, adding the wine and brandy when all are well blended. This should be made fully a fortnight before using, and well tied down to escape the air. If a more economical recipe is desired, use half the quantity of wine and brandy.

Lemon Conserve for Cheesecakes.

Ingredients.—¼ lb. fresh butter, 1 lb. powdered white sugar, 6 eggs, 3 large lemons.

Method.—Put the butter in a stew-pan, and, when dissolved, add the sugar, the yolks of six eggs and whites of *four*, well beaten, the grated rind and juice of three lemons. Stir the whole mixture over the fire until it is as thick as a good cream. Pot and tie down as for ordinary preserve, and the conserve will keep good for several months. When used, add a slice of bread soaked well in milk without the crust, and the milk strained off, or two sponge buns, or any light cake made into crumbs.

Orange Marmalade.

Ingredients.—To every pound of sliced fruit allow 3 pints of water; to every pound of pulp allow 1½ lb. of sugar.

Method.—Slice the oranges very thin without any preparation, and take out the pips. To each pound of sliced fruit add three pints of water; let it stand twenty-four hours. Boil it until the chips are tender; let it stand again twenty-four hours. Then weigh fruit and water together, and to every 1 lb. add 1½ lb. of sugar. Boil the whole until the sugar jellies and the chips are transparent—about an hour-and-a-half.

Ripe Gooseberry Jam.

Ingredients.—To every 1 lb. of fruit allow ¾ lb. of sugar. To every 6 lb. of fruit, ½ pint of red-currant juice.

Method.—Select red, hairy gooseberries, which should be gathered in dry weather, and when quite ripe. Weigh them, cut off the tops and tails, and to every 6 lb. of fruit add ½ a pint of redcurrant juice, drawn as for jelly. Put the fruit and juice into a preserving-pan, and let them boil rather quickly, keeping them well stirred. When they begin to break, which will be in about an hour, add the sugar, and keep simmering until it becomes firm, stirring and skimming all the time. Put it into pots (not too large), and when cold cover with oiled and egged paper.

Rhubarb Jam (Green).

Ingredients.—To 1½ lb. of green rhubarb allow 1 lb. loaf sugar, the thin rind of half a large lemon, ¼ oz. of bitter almonds, and a little ginger.

Method.—Wipe the rhubarb quite dry, cut it into pieces about two inches long, and put it into a preserving-pan with the sugar broken small; the rind of the lemon cut very fine, and the almonds blanched and divided. Boil the whole well together, taking care to stir and skim frequently, and when it is nearly done stir in the ginger. Young rhubarb will take about three-quarters of an hour, but if old it must be boiled for an hour-and-a-half. This preserve should be of a green colour, and will be found a very good substitute for greengage jam.

Rhubarb Jam (Red).

Ingredients.—4 lb. rhubarb—the red kind—4 lb. of loaf sugar, and 5 oz. whole ginger.

Method.—Peel and cut up the rhubarb into small pieces, add the sugar and ginger, and boil until clear. Pot and tie down as for other preserves. This should be of a brilliant red colour, and is very good for serving with blanc-mange, moulded rice, or rice flummery.

ADDITIONAL RECIPES.

SOUPS.

Onion Soup.

Ingredients.—2 or 3 large onions, 1½ pint of boiling milk, 3 potatoes, 1 pint boiling water, ½ oz. of butter, pepper and salt and toasted bread.

Method.—Put the butter in a saucepan, and when very hot add the onions sliced thin; stir and cook them till they are red, then add half a teacupful of flour. Stir this also until red, watching that it does not burn. Then add the boiling water, pepper and salt, mix them well in, let it boil a minute, then pour it into the soup kettle and let it stand on the back of the range till almost time to serve. Now add the boiling milk and have ready three well-boiled mashed potatoes. Add to the potatoes a little of the soup at first, then more until they are smooth and thin enough to pour into the soup kettle. Stir all well and smoothly together, taste to see if it is well seasoned with pepper and salt, as it requires plenty, especially of the latter. Let it simmer a few minutes, put pieces of toasted bread cut diamond shape into the tureen, pour the soup over them and serve very hot.

Rabbit Soup.

Ingredients.—1 rabbit, 3 onions, 1 carrot, 1 turnip, pepper corns and salt, 2 quarts of water.

Method.—Wash the rabbit and cut it up, and stew it with the vegetables till the meat will slip from the bones. Press the meat and vegetables through a colander, return them to the stock, season with pepper and salt, boil up once and serve.

Note.—This dish may be varied by adding to it a little curry powder and a cup of boiled rice.

Potato Soup.—No. 2.

Ingredients.—7 or 8 potatoes, 1 onion, butter or dripping, 3 pints of water, 1 large tablespoon of chopped parsley, the yolks of two eggs, pepper and salt.

Method.—Fry the potatoes and onion in the butter or dripping, when they are slightly coloured put them into the boiling water, and add the parsley. Let it boil till the potatoes are quite soft, then press all through a colander. Return the purée to the fire and let it simmer for two or three minutes;

when just time to serve, have ready the yolks of eggs well beaten; add to them a small quantity of the soup, stirring all the time; when mixed, add them gradually to the hot soup, with plenty of pepper and salt. Do not let the soup *boil* after the eggs are in, or they will curdle.

Vegetable Purée.

Ingredients.—Onions, carrots, potatoes (boiled first), beans of any kind, parsnips, celery, peas, leek turnips, cauliflower, &c.

Method.—Cut up a large plateful of any and all kinds of vegetables you happen to have—always having potatoes or beans for thickening. First, put into a saucepan a tea-cup of dripping or stock-fat, and when very hot add the sliced onions; stir well to prevent them burning, and when they are red, stir in a large spoonful of flour till it is of the same colour. Now stir in a pint of hot water and some pepper and salt—mind *not* to add the pepper and salt at first, as the onions and flour would then more readily burn. Now add the rest of the vegetables, and let them simmer, adding more hot water as necessary, for two hours; then press them through a colander, return them to the range and let them simmer till the moment of serving.

FISH AND MEAT.

Canapées of Sardines.

Ingredients.—Sardines, the yolks of three or four hard-boiled eggs, a little butter, mustard, pepper, and vinegar, slices of toast.

Method.—Take some slices of roll and cut them neatly into oval or octagon shapes. Toast them slightly, or fry them in oil or butter till they are of a nice yellow colour. Take some sardines, and strip them from the bones: lay one-half of them aside, and pound the other to a smooth paste with the eggs and butter. Add the mustard, pepper, and vinegar. When these ingredients are well mixed, spread the paste over the prepared slices of toast. On the top lay the other half of the sardines, cut into small strips, stand them in a Dutch oven before the fire and serve very hot.

Sardines on Toast.

Ingredients.—Sardines, cayenne, and lemon juice.

Method.—Scrape and bone the sardines, lay them on a plate; sprinkle them with lemon juice and a little cayenne pepper. Stand them in the oven until thoroughly hot: have ready some neat slices of hot-buttered toast; lay the sardines on these and serve at once.

Note.—This dish may be varied by spreading the toast with anchovy paste before laying on the sardines.

Soles in Batter.

Ingredients.—1 pair of soles, not very thick, pepper and salt; for the batter, ½ lb. of flour, 2 ozs. butter, ½ teaspoonful of salt, 2 eggs, enough milk to mix it; lard or dripping for frying.

Method.—Fillet the soles, and cut each fillet in two pieces, that they may not be too large, and sprinkle them with pepper and salt. Make a light batter with the above ingredients, taking care that it is not very thin; dip each piece of fish into this, and fry quickly in boiling fat to a golden brown. Arrange them in a circle, one overlapping the other, on a hot dish, and garnish with fresh or fried parsley. They are best served as soon as cooked. Melted butter may be sent to table with them in a tureen, if liked.

American Fritters.

Ingredients.—Slices of undercooked roast beef or mutton; for the batter, ½ lb. flour, 1 large or two small eggs, salt, milk; lard or dripping for frying.

Method.—Cut the meat into moderately thick slices, and as neat a shape as possible, pepper and salt each piece, then make a batter in the above proportions, taking care that it is not *very* thin. Have ready a pan of boiling lard or dripping, dip each piece of meat into the batter, and fry quickly to a light brown. Serve on a hot dish, and garnish with a thick border of fried apples.

Boiled Brains.

Ingredients.—Calf's or bullock's brains, pepper and salt, marjoram or sage, sippets of toasted bread.

Method.—Steep the brains in lukewarm water for two hours to draw the blood, then tie in muslin, put into boiling water and boil for 20 minutes; take them up, drain in a colander, then turn into a basin and beat thoroughly with a fork, season with plenty of pepper and salt and a little marjoram or sage—sage is best. Put on a hot dish, pour over a good melted butter sauce, and garnish with sippets of toast. This makes a good breakfast or supper dish. Care must be taken in preparing it to have all the basins and dishes *very hot*.

Roulades of Beef.

Ingredients.—Slices of undercooked roast beef, slices of boiled ham, 1 egg, pepper and mustard, a little thick gravy, fine crumbs; butter or dripping for frying.

Method.—Cut the beef into thin, even, oblong

slices, the ham rather thinner and smaller; spread one side of the beef with mustard, and pepper the ham. Lay the ham upon the beef and roll up together as lightly as possible; brush over with the egg, roll each in the crumbs, and pierce through with a slender skewer in such a manner as to keep the roll pinned together. Put several on each skewer, but do not let them touch one another; fry brown, lay on a hot dish, and gently withdraw the skewers, then pour the gravy boiling hot over them, and serve. Small roulades are a nice garnish for game and roast poultry.

Beef Olives.

Ingredients.—Slices of under-cooked roast beef, breadcrumbs, sweet herbs, pepper and salt, and gravy.

Method.—Cut the slices of meat very thin, spread upon each slice a stuffing made from the above ingredients, roll up tightly, and tie with string. Have ready in a saucepan some good brown gravy, lay in the olives, and let them simmer for about half an hour. Take up, remove the string carefully that the shape may not be spoiled, pour the gravy over, and serve hot.

Veal Shape.

Ingredients.—1½ lbs. of veal, 1 lemon, 1 slice of ham, pepper and salt, 3 hard-boiled eggs.

Method.—Stew the meat, with the thin rind of the lemon, in a very little water till quite tender. When done, cut up both veal and ham into small pieces, mince the lemon rind finely, and set these aside to cool. Strain the stock, add the lemon juice and seasonings, and let this also cool. Cut the eggs into slices, and arrange them in a plain mould or dish, pour in the cool stock and meat, and set aside till quite cold, when it should turn out whole. This makes an excellent breakfast dish.

Stewed Steak and Macaroni.

Ingredients.—1½ lbs. of steak, or other lean beef, a little flour, butter for frying, 1 tablespoonful of ketchup, ¼ lb. macaroni.

Method.—Cut the beef in small pieces, roll it in the flour, and fry slightly in a little butter; put it into a stewpan, cover with hot water, and allow it to simmer slowly for 1½ hours; then add the macaroni, and simmer again for three quarters of an hour; season with pepper, salt, and ketchup, and stew for 10 minutes after the seasoning is added. Serve on a hot dish, the beef in the centre, and the macaroni round.

Swiss Pâtés.

Ingredients.—Remains of cold roast veal or fowl, a little white sauce, rounds of stale bread, 1 egg, (well beaten), very fine breadcrumbs; good dripping or lard for frying.

Method.—Mince the meat finely, well season it with some of the forcemeat or a little lemon peel, mix with thin white sauce, and set it near the fire to heat, stirring that it may not burn. Cut rather thick slices of bakers' bread into rounds with a cake cutter; with a smaller cutter extract a piece from the middle of each round, taking care not to let the sharp edge go quite through, but leaving enough in the cavity to serve as a bottom to the pâté. Dip the hollowed pieces of bread in the egg, strew them with fine crumbs, and fry in boiling fat to a delicate brown. Drain every drop of the fat from them by laying them on soft paper before the fire, then fill each with the hot mince, pile on a dish, garnish with parsley, and serve.

PUDDINGS AND SWEETS.

Alpine Pudding.

Ingredients.—A breakfast-cup of breadcrumbs, 1 dessert-spoonful of sugar, 1 dessert-spoonful of *finely chopped* suet, 1 pint of milk, 2 eggs, raspberry jam, a few drops of cochineal.

Method.—Mix the breadcrumbs, sugar and suet, put them in a pie-dish, and pour over them *nearly* a pint of boiling milk, then well whisk the yolks of the eggs and add them to the mixture; stir all well together and bake in a moderate oven till quite set, but not browned. Take it out, and when cool, *not cold*, cover the surface with a thin layer of raspberry preserve: then whip the whites of the eggs to a stiff froth—stiff enough to stand firmly—and with two forks pile it in rocky heaps upon the pudding; mix a few drops of cochineal with a large teaspoonful of the frothed whites, and lay this upon the snowy peaks in imitation of a sunset glow. Set it again in the oven for a few minutes to crisp, but do not let it brown, or both the appearance and flavour will be destroyed.

Apple Batter Pudding.

Ingredients.—3 good tablespoonfuls of flour, 2 eggs, 1 pint of milk, 1 tablespoonful of white pounded sugar, 3 large cooking apples.

Method.—Mix the flour to a smooth batter with the milk, then add the sugar and the eggs—which should be well beaten. Prepare the apples as for a pie, put them in a dish, pour the batter over them, and stir all together. Bake for an hour. A little grated lemon-peel is by some considered an improvement to the flavour of this pudding.

Apple Custard Pudding.

Ingredients.—Slices of bread, 3 or 4 juicy apples, 2 eggs, 1 pint of milk, 3 dessert-spoonfuls of sugar, $\frac{1}{2}$ teaspoonful of essence of lemon or vanilla.

Method.—Cut slices of bread about half an inch thick, and place a layer in the bottom of a deep pie-dish; next put a thin layer of apples—pared and sliced—then another layer of bread, and a thick top layer of apples. Beat the eggs well for five minutes, then add to them the sugar, flavouring, and milk, and pour this custard over the pudding. Place a dish over it, and let it soak for half-an-hour, then bake in a moderate oven.

Note.—Apples that will cook easily should be used for this recipe.

Apple Snow.—No. 1.

Ingredients.—$\frac{1}{4}$ lb. macaroons, $\frac{1}{2}$ pint of milk, 2 eggs, whites and yolks separate, 2 good apples raw, 2 tablespoonfuls of white pounded sugar.

Method.—Arrange the macaroons in a shallow glass dish, then make a boiled custard with the milk, the *yolks* of the eggs, and half the sugar, and pour over them while hot; stand this aside to cool and soak. When it is cold, whisk the eggs to a stiff froth, and stir in the rest of the sugar, before paring the apples. Peel and grate one apple directly into the *méringue* and whip in quickly, before touching the next. The pulp will better preserve its colour if thus coated before the air can affect it. It is well for one person to work in the apple while an assistant grates it. When the apple is well mixed in the *méringue*, pile this as lightly as possible upon the soaked macaroons, and set in a very cold place till wanted. It must be served soon after it is made.

Apple Snow.—No. 2.

Ingredients.—6 fine apples, 2 teacups of pounded sugar, juice of 1 lemon and a-half, the peel (grated), 1 pint of milk, 4 eggs.

Method.—Make a boiled custard of the milk, 1 cup of sugar, and the yolks of the eggs, and when cool pour it into a shallow glass dish. Bake the apples quite whole, in a covered dish, with a little water to prevent burning, till they are so tender that a straw will pierce them. Take off the skins and scrape out the pulp, taking care to avoid any pieces of core. Mix in the sugar and lemon, then beat the whites of the eggs to a stiff froth, and whip in the cold pulp by degrees till very white and firm. Pile this snow upon the custard and serve. If not used as soon as made, it should be set in a very cold place, or the snow will fall.

Apple Puffs.

Ingredients.—Apples, sugar to taste, good puff pastry.

Method.—Pare, quarter, core, and stew the apples with a *very little* water, till tender. When quite soft, take them out, beat to a smooth pulp, sweeten to taste, and set aside to cool. Roll out the pastry about a ¼ of an inch thick and cut into squares 3 inches across. Brush round the edges with water or a little white of egg, lay in the centre a dessert-spoonful of the cool apple pulp, fold over quickly, cornerwise, gently press the edges together and bake in a brisk oven about 15 minutes.

Bachelor's Pudding (No. 2).

Ingredients.—2 large tablespoonfuls of flour, 2 large tablespoonfuls of finely-chopped suet, 1 salt-spoonful of salt, enough milk or water to make a very stiff batter.

Method.—Mix the above ingredients well together; then dip a pudding-cloth in boiling water, wring nearly dry, sprinkle with flour, and tie the pudding rather tightly in it. Boil from 1½ to two hours, and serve with good gravy.

Note.—A *large* pudding made in the above proportions is equally good, and for children may be served with jam or golden syrup. Boil for three hours.

Cup Puddings.

Ingredients.—3 ozs. butter, 3 ozs. flour, 2 ozs. powdered sugar, ¼ pint of milk.

Method.—Beat the butter to a cream, add the sugar, stir in the flour, and mix with the milk. Bake in buttered cups for about half an hour. Serve with sweet sauce.

Fig Pudding.—No. 3. (Without Eggs).

Ingredients.—½ lb. suet, ½ lb. flour, ½ lb. figs, ¼ lb. moist sugar, ½ oz. of baking powder, enough milk or water to mix the pudding.

Method.—Mix the baking powder with the flour, chop the suet *very fine*, cut up the figs into small pieces, add the sugar, and mix all the dry ingredients well together, add enough milk to moisten them, and boil *at once* in a basin or mould for three hours.

Free Kirk Pudding.

Ingredients.—Two tablespoonfuls each of raisins, currants, sugar, breadcrumbs, ground rice, and flour, 3 tablespoonfuls of finely chopped suet, ½ teaspoonful of mixed spice, ¼ teaspoonful of carbonate of soda, a little candied orange peel, a small pinch of salt, and a little milk.

Method.—Stone the raisins, wash and pick over the currants, rub the breadcrumbs quite fine, and chop the suet well; then stir all the dry ingredients well together, and mix with a little milk in which the soda has been dissolved. Boil in a buttered mould or basin for two hours.

Gingerbread Cup Puddings.

Ingredients.—¼ lb. suet—finely minced—6 ozs. flour, 2 ozs. breadcrumbs, 1 teaspoonful baking powder, 3 tablespoonfuls brown sugar, 1 tablespoonful of ground ginger, a pinch of salt, ½ lb. treacle, 1 egg, a little milk.

Method.—Mix all the dry ingredients well together; beat the egg, add a little milk, and mix the pudding with this and the treacle, working it well together with a spoon. Well butter some cups, half fill them with the mixture, cover with greased paper, and *steam* for three quarters of an hour. The above recipe may be used for one large pudding, but it will then require to be steamed for 2½ hours.

German Pancakes.

Ingredients.—Half-pint of milk, a pinch of salt, 2 ozs. butter, 1 dessert-spoonful of white sugar, 6 ozs. flour, 3 eggs, well beaten.

Method.—Put the milk over the fire in a saucepan, with the salt, butter, and sugar, and as it warms add (by degrees) the flour, stirring, that it does not become lumpy. When it thickens, turn out and add the eggs, and beat well together. Have ready a pan of boiling fat, drop in a teaspoonful at a time, and fry to a light brown. They should be of a nice, round shape, and very light. Serve with sifted sugar or jam. The above quantity makes a large dish.

Jam Puffs.

Ingredients.—Good puff paste, jam—raspberry or greengage is best.

Method.—Roll out the pastry till about a ¼ of an inch thick and cut into squares 3 inches across, brush round the edges with a little white of egg, put a large teaspoonful of preserve in the centre, fold over cornerwise, gently press the edges together and bake for about 15 minutes in a brisk oven. If greengage jam is used, the stones should be taken out before it is put into the puffs.

Sir Watkin Wynne Pudding.

Ingredients.—6 ozs. minced suet, 12 ozs. grated bread, 4 eggs, 8 ozs. pounded sugar, 3 tablespoonfuls of marmalade, and milk. For the sauce—peel of half a lemon, 6 lumps of sugar, 1 teacup of water.

Method.—Mix the suet, bread, and marmalade, add the well-beaten eggs, with which should be mixed the sugar, add a little milk, beat well, and boil in a buttered mould 2½ hours. Cut the lemon-peel into very fine straws, put them in a small saucepan with the sugar and water, simmer together for twenty minutes, then pour over the pudding, leaving the " straws " on the top. The quantity of sugar in the pudding may be reduced by those who do not care for much sweetness.

Thorpe Pudding.

Ingredients.—Breadcrumbs, 2 eggs, 1 pint of milk, 1 tablespoonful of sugar, greengage or blackcurrant jam.

Method.—Put a tolerably thick layer of jam in he bottom of a small pie-dish, and place on the to of it a layer of fine breadcrumbs about an inch thick. Well whisk the eggs, add the sugar, then the milk, and pour this custard very gently over the crumbs, so as not to disturb them, grate a little nutmeg over the top, and bake from 20 to 30 minutes. It should be quite a light brown. This pudding is sometimes made with an edge of pastry round the dish, which improves its appearance.

Wafer Puddings.

Ingredients.—1½ oz. fresh butter, 2 oz. flour, 2 eggs, ½ pint of milk, jam.

Method.—Work the butter into the flour, add the eggs, previously well beaten, then the milk, and mix all well together. Have ready five or six well-buttered saucers; pour a part of the mixture into each and bake at once in a tolerably quick oven, till of a delicate brown colour, about half an hour. When done, turn out, spread each one with jam, and fold over like a pasty. They must be served as soon as ready.

Lemon Cheesecakes.

Ingredients.—2 ozs. of butter, 2 ozs. of powdered sugar, 2 eggs, yolks and whites beaten separately, 1 dessert-spoonful of ground rice, the rind and juice of 2 lemons.

Method.—Put the butter and sugar in a jar or jug, and stand that in a saucepan of boiling water. Stir till all is melted, then add the ground rice and lemon rind, juice, and eggs; keep stirring it till it thickens. Line patty pans with paste and put the mixture in. They must not be cooked in too hot an oven.

Custards.

Ingredients.—1 pint of milk, 2 ozs. of loaf sugar, 3 bitter almonds blanched and pounded, 3 *whole* eggs, or the yolks of 4.

Method.—Put the milk, with the sugar and almonds, on the fire and when hot, *but not boiling*, pour gently in the eggs, well beaten. Then pour the mixture into a jug, stand the jug in a *deep* saucepan of boiling water and stir till it thickens. Serve in custard cups.

Gooseberry Jelly.

Ingredients.—To every quart of berries allow 1 pint of water. To every pint of juice allow 1lb. of sugar.

Method.—Stew the gooseberries in the above proportion of water till the fruit is quite broken, and while hot strain through a sieve, but do not press the fruit, or the jelly will not be clear. Boil the strained juice with the sugar for twenty minutes, or till it will jelly on a plate. It should be a pretty pink colour. The gooseberries left will make a good jam for common use, with the addition of 1lb. of sugar to each pound of fruit.

Dinner for an Invalid.

A STEWED CHOP.

Ingredients.—A good chop from a loin of mutton, 2 tablespoonfuls of water, salt.

Method.—Trim all the fat from the meat and put it in a covered jar (a salt jar does very well for the purpose) with the water; stand it in a moderately hot oven, let it steam for half an hour, and a few minutes before serving, add a pinch of salt. Serve very hot, with the gravy poured over it. Steak or chops cooked in this manner are very tender and easily digested.

INVALID PUDDING.

Ingredients.—2 tablespoonfuls of breadcrumbs, 1 egg, nearly ½ a pint of milk, a little sugar, *flavouring* if liked.

Method.—Mix all well together pour into a buttered cup or mould, and boil half an hour. This is also a nice pudding for a child.

CUP CUSTARD.

Ingredients.—1 egg, ½ a breakfastcup of new milk, 1 dessert-spoonful of white pounded sugar.

Method.—Stir the sugar into the milk, add the egg, which should be well beaten; pour into a breakfast cup and bake till quite set—about a quarter of an hour. Turn out on a plate and serve alone, or with a little stewed fruit.

ODDS AND ENDS.

Recipe for Making Coffee.

An Indian Coffee Planter sends us the following recipe, with the desire that it may be useful to the promoters of temperance. "I do not know," he remarks, "what rubbish people may use in England under the name of coffee, but of course take for granted that genuine decent coffee will be used in testing the recipe."

The directions must be strictly adhered to.

1. The coffee should be roasted just before use; as if kept more than one day after roasting there is a decided oss of aroma.

2. The simplest way of roasting coffee is in an

enamelled frying-pan. Roast the beans over a *mild, smokeless* fire until the beans turn a rich brown colour, *not* black. The beans must be constantly stirred and turned, or they will burn.

3. Take one large tablespoonful of coffee *powder* for each cup of coffee required.

4. Put the powder into a jug and pour *boiling* water over it in the proportion of half a cupful of water to each tablespoonful of coffee powder. The water must be at *full* boiling point.

5. Let the coffee stand in the jug for half an hour, and then strain through a *linen* or *cotton* bag (muslin is too thin) into the coffee-pot.

6. To *one quarter* of a cupful of coffee add three-fourths of *boiling* milk, and sugar to taste.

Frosted Vegetables.

To extract the frost, prepare them for cooking, and lay in cold salted water all night, standing the vessel in which they are placed in a warm room. The water must quite cover them.

BRAND & CO.'S SPECIALTIES FOR INVALIDS

CONCENTRATED BEEF TEA, VEAL, MUTTON & CHICKEN BROTHS; TURTLE SOUP & JELLY, CALFS' FOOT JELLY, MEAT LOZENGES, &c.

ESSENCES OF BEEF, MUTTON, VEAL AND CHICKEN

BRAND & CO.'S
INVALID SOUPS, POTTED MEATS, PRESERVED PROVISIONS, &c., &c.

A FINE TONIC AND DIGESTIVE.
Each Article Manufactured from Materials of the very best Quality.
Caution—Beware of Imitations.

Sole Address—No. 11, Little Stanhope St., Hertford St., Mayfair, London, W.

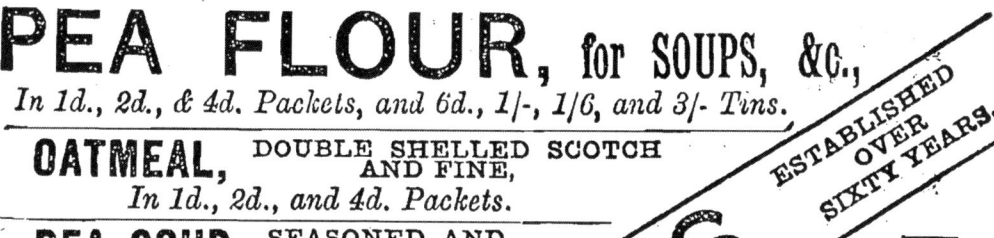

SYMINGTON'S
ESTABLISHED OVER SIXTY YEARS.

PEA FLOUR, for SOUPS, &c.,
In 1d., 2d., & 4d. Packets, and 6d., 1/-, 1/6, and 3/- Tins.

OATMEAL, DOUBLE SHELLED SCOTCH AND FINE,
In 1d., 2d., and 4d. Packets.

PEA SOUP, SEASONED AND FLAVOURED,
In 1d. & 2d. Packets, & 3d., 6d. & 1/- Tins.

EGYPTIAN FOOD.
A preparation of FINEST EGYPTIAN LENTILS and other nutritious substances. Used extensively in preference to any other at Smedley's Hydropathic Establishment, Matlock Bank, Derbyshire.
In Tins, 1s. per lb.

ARAB'S COFFEE,
In Oblong Tins, 1 lb. ½lb., and ¼lb., 1/10 per lb.

DANDELION COFFEE.
Breakfast Beverage. For Persons of Weak Digestion and those suffering from Liver Complaints, this is Invaluable.
In Tins, 6d., 1s., and 1s. 6d. each.

PATENTEES AND MANUFACTURERS.

W. SYMINGTON & CO.,
Bowden Steam Mills,
MARKET HARBOROUGH,
And 16, Ludgate Hill, London.

LAMPLOUGH'S PYRETIC SALINE

Have it in your Houses, for it is the true Antidote in
Small-pox, Fevers, Eruptive Affections, Sea or Bilious Sickness, Headache, Nausea, Constipation, Indigestion, Heartburn, and Thirst, and has abundant medical testimony to its invaluable properties, especially in Fevers and Blood Poisons.

CAUTION.—Beware of worthless Salines containing injurious matter put forward in imitation of **Pyretic Saline** by unprincipled persons at the risk of the health of the public.

Pyretic Saline is warranted not to contain magnesia or any substance likely to produce Gallstones or Calculous formations.

May be obtained of all Chemists, and the Proprietor,
In Bottles, 2/6, 4/6, 11/-, and 21/- each.

H. LAMPLOUGH, Consulting Chemist, 113, Holborn, E.C.

VALUABLE FAMILY MEDICINE.
ESTABLISHED 1835.

WHELPTON'S VEGETABLE PURIFYING PILLS,

Are one of those rare Medicines which, for their extraordinary properties, have gained an almost UNIVERSAL REPUTATION. Numbers are constantly bearing testimony to their great value in Disorders of the **Head, Chest, Bowels, Liver,** and **Kidneys;** also in **Rheumatism,** as may be seen from the Testimonials published from time to time. By the timely use of such a remedy many of the seriously afflicting disorders which result from proper means being neglected might be avoided and much suffering saved, for "PREVENTION IS BETTER THAN CURE."

Sold in Boxes, price 7½d., 1s. 1½d., and 2s. 9d., by **G. WHELPTON & SON, 3, Crane Court, Fleet Street, London.** and by Chemists and Medicine Vendors at Home and Abroad. Sent free by post in the United Kingdom for 8, 14, or 33 stamps.

LINCOLNSHIRE FEATHER BEDS.

The LINCOLNSHIRE FEATHER BED CO. (Regd.)
ARE NOW OFFERING THEIR

Well-known **FEATHER BEDS** at the following Reduced Prices:—
No. 1.—SINGLE BED, BOLSTER, and PILLOW, 6-ft. 6-in. by 3-ft. 6-in., weighing 40 lbs. 30/0
No. 2.—DOUBLE BED, BOLSTER, and 2 PILLOWS, 6-ft. 6-in. by 4-ft. 6-in., weighing 50 lbs. ... 37/6
No. 3.—DOUBLE BED, BOLSTER, and 2 PILLOWS, 6-ft. 6-in. by 4-ft. 6-in., weighing 55 lbs. ... 41/3
No. 4.—EXTRA SIZED BED, BOLSTER, and 2 PILLOWS, 6-ft. 6-in. by 5-ft., weighing 63 lbs. 47/3
WARRANTED NEW, SWEET, AND FIT FOR IMMEDIATE USE.

Any-sized Bed only 9d. per lb., including Feathers, in best English Linen (bordered) Tick, making, packing, wrapper, and carriage paid to any station in the United Kingdom.
Samples of Feathers and Tick, Price List, &c., post free.
All Orders must be accompanied by Cheque or P.O.O., made payable to the Manager, H. STEVENS, 178, Strand, which, to ensure safe delivery of Goods, may be post-dated ten days. P.O.O. payable Chief Office, London.
SUPERIOR BEDS, OF SPLENDID FEATHERS AND LINEN TICKS, 1s. per lb. Samples free.

H. STEVENS, 178, STRAND, LONDON, W.C.,
Where Beds may be seen and obtained. Please mention this Book.

OLDRIDGE'S BALM of COLUMBIA
(ESTABLISHED SIXTY YEARS).

Is the best and only certain remedy ever discovered for Preserving, Strengthening, Beautifying, or Restoring the **HAIR, WHISKERS,** or **MOUSTACHES,** and preventing them turning gray.

Price 3s. 6d., 6s., and 11s. per Bottle.

C. & A. OLDRIDGE,
22, Wellington Street, Strand, London, W.C.
AND ALL CHEMISTS AND PERFUMERS.

For Children it is invaluable, as it forms the basis of a magnificent head of hair, and prevents baldness in mature age.

MAGNETINE.

These Appliances are recommended and used by the Profession for the Cure of

Gout	Asthma	Chest Weakness	Sore Throat
Sciatica	Rheumatism	Spinal Affections	Heart Affections
Lumbago	Rheumatic Gout	Bronchitis	Liver Complaint
Neuralgia	Lung Affections	Winter Cough	General Debility

And every other form of Nervousness and Rheumatic Affection.

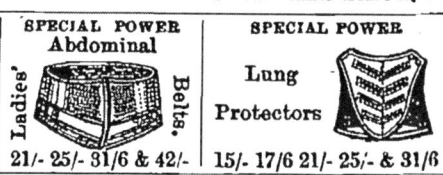

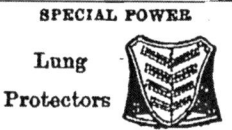

SPECIAL POWER Stomach Appliances.	SPECIAL POWER Ladies' Abdominal Belts.	SPECIAL POWER Lung Protectors	SPECIAL POWER Knee Caps.
7/6 10/6 & 12/6 each.	21/- 25/- 31/6 & 42/-	15/- 17/6 21/- 25/- & 31/6	5/3 6/3 & 7/6

Mr. DARLOW,   Lewisham, 6th July, 1880.

Dear Sir,—Will you please forward me a Magnetine Band, according to the enclosed measurement? And I will take this opportunity of informing you that I have frequently recommended your Appliances to friends suffering from neuralgia. For I have received the greatest possible benefit from them myself where all other remedies have failed to alleviate the pain. You are at liberty to make what use you please of this letter, for I have always been thankful to the friend who recommended me to try "Magnetine," and shall be glad to render the same service to others.

Yours faithfully,   EMMA LESLIE,
Descriptive Pamphlet Post Free.   (Well known Authoress).

DARLOW & Co., 443, West Strand, LONDON.

THE PEOPLE'S GUIDE TO THE BEST NEW BOOKS.

THE LITERARY WORLD.

ONE PENNY.

BEST HOME JOURNAL.

THE FAMILY CIRCLE.

ONE PENNY.

BRIGHT TALES: WITTY SELECTIONS.

LONDON: JAMES CLARKE & CO., 13 & 14, FLEET ST., E.C.

WASHING-DAY REFORM.

BANISH the antiquated, absurd, and destructive process of rubbing and boiling the clothes, and adopt the easy common-sense plan with

HARPER TWELVETREES' VILLA WASHING MACHINE, £2 15s. (CASH PRICE £2 10s.)

OR WITH WRINGER AND MANGLER COMBINED, £5 5s. (CASH PRICE, £4 15s.)

Which is the Gem of all Washing Machines and does the Fortnight's Family Wash in Four Hours without Rubbing or Boiling, saving Five Hours of Copper Firing every Washing-day, as certified by Thousands of delighted "House-Mothers."

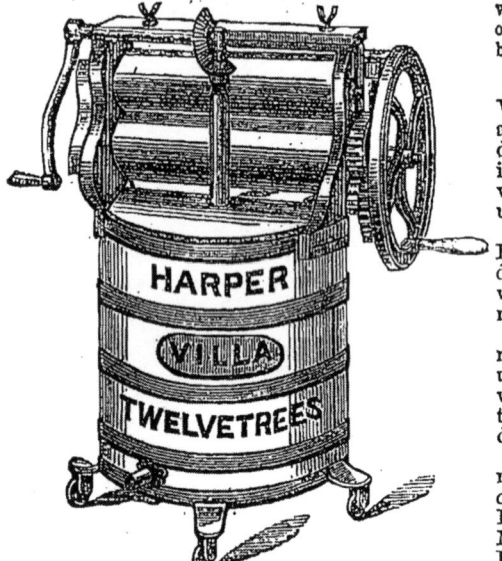

Mrs. WHITEWELL, Railway Cottage, Willesden, writes—"Your Villa Washer and Mangler is a wonderful machine. My daughter, aged fifteen, now does the washing for our family of twelve, in five hours, without any woman to help. We always used to have a woman two days."

Mrs. JONES, 16, Belgrave Gardens, Dover—" By following your printed directions in every detail, our washing, which formerly occupied a whole day is now easily done in two hours."

Mrs. TURNER, Fant, Maidstone—"I never thought anything could be half so useful. We have no trouble, and get our washing done in three hours, which before took a woman a whole day; and now we do without the washerwoman."

Carriage paid; free trial; easy instalment payments, or 10 per cent. cash discount. Illustrated Prospectus, 48 pp., from HARPER TWELVETREES, Laundry Machinist, 80, Finsbury Pavement, London, E.C. Works: Burdett Road, Bow, E.

BRUCE'S OIL COOKING STOVES.

THE "HOUSEHOLD FRIEND."

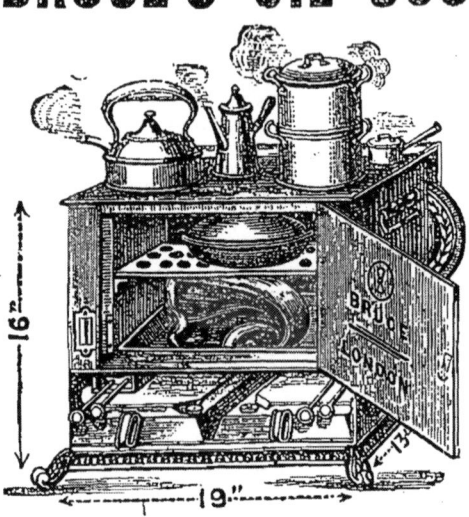

The Latest and most Improved Stove to Roast, Bake several articles in oven at once, Boil, Fry, or Steam, and Warm Plates at one time; will cook a dinner, three courses, for six persons, in three hours—cost TWOPENCE. Complete, with 6-pint kettle, 6-pint saucepan and steamer, fry-pan, meat-tray, and grid, plate warmer, two baking covers, centre movable tray, funnel, and pair steel scissors; packed in strong box (which forms a good stand for stove afterwards)

35/- Complete with all Utensils. 35/-

The only Stove of its size yet invented with Centre Movable Tray and Plate Warmer.

Bazaar says: "Having thoroughly tested it, we have no hesitation in recommending it as trustworthy and well-finished, all complete, being only 35s., making it a marvel of cheapness, and the BEST STOVE of its Size and Price in the MARKET. Mr. Bruce offers, with great fairness, to change the stove or return the money if not approved of."

NOTICE TO COUNTRY RESIDENTS.—No extra charge for Packing or Boxes; free, delivered to all principal London railway stations. The only firm trading with such exceptional terms.

Send for Illustrated Price List, Testimonials, &c., Post-free to any Part of the World.

R. C. BRUCE 90, BLACKMAN ST., LONDON, S.E.

BENETFINK & CO.'S
ELECTRO-PLATE, CUTLERY, & FURNISHING IRONMONGERY GALLERIES,
107 & 108, CHEAPSIDE (opposite Bow Church), & 89 & 90, CHEAPSIDE.

GOG
The Giants, 8ft. 6in. high, guard the Entrance.

MAGOG
The Giants, 8ft. 6in. high, guard the Entrance.

BENETFINK and CO.'S ELECTRO-SILVER PLATE is unequalled for Beauty of Design, Fineness of Finish, and Low Prices.

BENETFINK and CO.'S TABLE-KNIVES are Matchless for Quality and Price.

BENETFINK and CO.'S STOCK of FENDERS, STOVES, and FIRE IRONS is Elegant and Cheap.

BENETFINK and CO.'S STOCK of GAS CHANDELIERS and LAMPS for Home and Foreign use.

BENETFINK and CO.'S IRON BEDSTEADS are new in Design and Simple in Construction.

BENETFINK and CO.'S STOCK of BEDROOM FURNITURE and BEDDING is of the Best Manufacture.

BENETFINK and CO.'S STOCK contains BATHS of every Shape and Description.

BENETFINK and CO. SELL the very best Articles, and Charge the very Lowest Prices.

5 per cent. and carriage paid to any part of the Kingdom.

Catalogues, with 1,000 Engravings, sent Gratis and Post Free.

5 lbs. Feathers to be Given Away, Suitable for Cushions, Pillows, &c.

NEW FEATHER BEDS at HALF-PRICE

Annual Sale, over 3,000 Beds.

Carriage Paid to any Station.

Branches:—LINCOLN and LONDON.

FEATHERS COLLECTED FROM ALL PARTS OF LINCOLNSHIRE.

THE LINCOLNSHIRE BEDDING COMPANY have sold thousands of their Feather Beds during the past few months. The Feathers are specially purified by steam. No chemicals are used.

As an evidence of good faith, all Cheques or Post Office Orders may be post-dated ten days to ensure proper delivery of the Goods, and the Company guarantee to pay cost of Bed, and pay carriage both ways if the Goods are not as described.

The "ROYAL" Double Bed, 6ft. 6in. long, by 5ft. wide, 65lbs. in weight; two pillows, one bolster ... ... 65s.

The "WINDSOR" Double Bed, 6ft. 6in. long, by 4ft. 6in. wide, 55lbs. in weight; two pillows, one bolster ... ... 55s.

The "PALACE" Double Bed, 6ft. 6in. long, by 4ft. 6in. wide, 50lbs. in weight; two pillows, one bolster ... ... 50s.

The "COTTAGE" Single Bed, 6ft. 6in. long, by 3ft. 6in. wide, 40lbs. in weight; one pillow, one bolster ... ... 40s.

Packing and Wrapper free with each Bed.

All orders must be accompanied by Cheque or P. O. O. payable to London Agent, Mr. T. SMITH, 15, Wine Office Court, Fleet Street, E.C., where Specimen Beds may be seen. P.O.O. payable at Ludgate Circus. Cheques crossed City Bank. Please say where you saw this Advertisement.

SPARKLING HYGEIA.

This most successful beverage ever introduced achieves in perfection what alcoholic mixtures only pretend to do. It is a real stimulant, a true nerve tonic, dissipating languor, and wonderfully increasing energy and *verve*. To brain-workers it is inestimable.

"Ought to be on every dinner-table." "Leeds, July 29, 1889.

"'Sparkling Hygeia' is a most agreeable and exhilarating tonic beverage, well deserving public appreciation and support. "CLARENCE FOSTER, M.R.C.S.,

"Member du Congrès International d'Hygiène à Turin."

"In taste and appearance it resembles a mild champagne; while perfectly unintoxicating, it possesses the qualities of an exhilarating and refreshing beverage."—*Christian World.*

Sample Case of One Dozen on receipt of 6s.

Sole Proprietor—R. McDOUGALL, Washington Hotel, Liverpool,

AND 61, ST. PAUL'S CHURCHYARD, LONDON.

"THE WASHINGTON,"
LIVERPOOL.

The Largest and Best Temperance Hotel in the World.

First-class Bedroom, Attendance, Breakfast, and Tea,
8s. per Day. Commercial Charge, 7s. per Day.

SPECIALLY RESERVED ROOMS. 1/6 EXTRA.

THOMAS BRADFORD & CO., LAUNDRY ENGINEERS AND DOMESTIC MACHINISTS.

KNIFE CLEANERS.	BUTTER CHURNS.	"VOWEL" WASHING MACHINES.	WRINGING AND MANGLING MACHINES.	LAUNDRY STOVES.	LAWN MOWERS.
CINDER SIFTERS.	BUTTER WORKERS.			POLISHING IRONS.	GARDEN SEATS.
BONE MILLS.	MILK PAILS.			LINEN PRESSES.	GARDEN REQUISITES
CASK STANDS.	CHEESE PRESSES.			DRYING CLOSETS.	CORN CRUSHERS.
SAUSAGE MACHINES.	DAIRY REQUISITES	BOOT CLEANERS.	SEWING MACHINES.	LAUNDRY REQUISITES	CHAFF CUTTERS.

140 to 143, High Holborn, LONDON.
Manchester and Liverpool.
CATALOGUE FREE.

A FEW RECIPES FOR USING

Borwick's Gold Medal Baking Powder.

To make Bread.—To every pound of flour add a *large heaped-up teaspoonful* of Borwick's Baking Powder, with a little salt, and *thoroughly mix* while in a dry state, then pour on gradually about half a pint of *cold* water, or milk and water, mixing quickly but thoroughly into a dough of the usual consistence, taking care not to knead it more than is necessary to mix it perfectly; make it into *small* loaves, which must be *immediately* put into a *quick oven*.

Puff Paste.—Mix one pound of flour with a teaspoonful of *Borwick's Baking Powder*, then cut half a pound of butter into slices, roll it in thin sheets on some of your flour, wet up the rest with about a quarter of a pint of water, see that it is about as stiff as your butter, roll it to a thin sheet, cover it with your sheets of butter, double it in a three double; do the same five times, it is then fit for use, or it may stand an hour covered over to keep the air from it.

Plum Cakes.—One pound of flour, a teaspoonful and a-half of *Borwick's Baking Powder*, a little salt, quarter of a pound each of butter, sugar, and currants, two eggs and half a pint of milk.

Pancakes.—One pound of flour, one teaspoonful of *Borwick's Baking Powder*, and a little salt, mix well *dry*; add an egg or two beaten up, and sufficient milk to make a thin batter, and fry at once with lard or butter.

Apple Pancakes.—Half a teaspoonful of *Borwick's Baking Powder*, and a little salt, to two tablespoonfuls of flour, add two eggs well beaten, and enough milk to make a smooth and rather thin batter, then take a little powdered cinnamon, grated lemon peel, two ounces of currants, and six apples peeled and chopped; mix well together; melt some butter in a frying pan, and do not put the mixture in till quite hot.

CUSTARDS WITHOUT EGGS!
BORWICK'S CUSTARD POWDER,

For making delicious Custards in less time, and at one-half of the usual expense. This valuable substitute should be in every household. When prepared with fruit, it forms a truly refreshing and *recherché* dish. For Blanc-Mange it is particularly recommended.

DIRECTIONS FOR USE.

From a pint of new milk take two tablespoonfuls and mix up with one ounce of this Powder, cold; sweeten the remainder of the milk to your taste, and pour on when it fully boils, stirring quickly.

BLANC-MANGE.—Same as for Custards, with less milk.

A Cheap and Ready TABLE DELICACY always at hand.

In 1d. and 2d. Packets, and 6d. and 1s. Tins. Sold by all Grocers, Corndealers, &c.

KOPF'S EXTRACT of MEAT COMPANY,

LIMITED.

FIRST PRIZE GOLD MEDAL

AT THE

SYDNEY EXHIBITION of 1879

FOR

"Extracts of Meat and Nutritious Preparations generally."

KOPF'S EXTRACT OF BEEF,
The purest and most nutritious form of Beef Tea.

KOPF'S ESSENCE OF BEEF,
Especially adapted for Invalids with weak digestion.

KOPF'S BEEF LOZENGES,
Invaluable to those who have to fast long.

KOPF'S CONSOLIDATED SOUPS
Of Erbswurst or Pea Soup, Mulligatawny, Green Pea, Scotch Broth, Hotch Potch, Lentil, &c., 2d. to 4d. each tin. In cases, Mock Turtle, Oxtail, Julienne, Chicken and Rice, and Curries (Chicken and Rabbit, Turtle, clear and thick, &c.).

KOPF'S PREPARED MARROW,
From best Beef Marrow Bones. KOPF'S EXQUISITE BISCUITS.

KOPF'S COMPRESSED VEGETABLES,
Preserving the characteristics of fresh vegetables. Children's and Invalid's Food. Jellies and Calf's Foot Gelatine.

KOPF'S CONSOLIDATED TEA and COFFEE,
With and without milk and sugar.

Patronised by the Nobility and Gentry, the Army and Navy, Sportsmen, Yachtsmen, Tourists, &c.

KOPF'S EXTRACT of MEAT COMPANY,
LIMITED.

2, DRAPER'S GARDENS, LONDON, E.C.